IT Governance based on COBIT®

CW00408857

Other publications by Van Haren Publishing

Van Haren Publishing (VHP) specializes in titles on Best Practices, methods and standards within four domains:
- IT management,
- Architecture (Enterprise and IT),
- Business management and
- Project management

These publications are grouped in series: *ITSM Library, Best Practice* and *IT Management Topics*. VHP is also publisher on behalf of leading companies and institutions: The Open Group, IPMA-NL, PMI-NL, CA, Getronics, Quint, The Sox Institute and ASL BiSL Foundation

Topics are (per domain):

IT (Service) Management / IT Governance	Architecture (Enterprise and IT)	Project/Programme/ Risk Management
ASL	Archimate®	A4-Projectmanagement
BiSL	GEA®	ICB / NCB
CATS	TOGAF™	MINCE®
CMMI		M_o_R®
CobiT	**Business Management**	MSP™
ISO 17799	EFQM	PMBOK® Guide
ISO 27001	ISA-95	PRINCE2™
ISO 27002	ISO 9000	
ISO/IEC 20000	ISO 9001:2000	
ISPL	SixSigma	
IT Service CMM	SOX	
ITIL® V2	SqEME®	
ITIL® V3		
ITSM		
MOF		
MSF		
ABC of ICT		

For the latest information on VHP publications, visit our website: www.vanharen.net.

IT Governance based on COBIT® 4.1

A Management Guide

Van Haren
PUBLISHING

Colophon

Title:	IT Governance based on CobiT® 4.1 - A Management Guide
Authors:	Koen Brand (Steenbok Adviesgroep, the Netherlands) & Harry Boonen (Boonen Consultancy & Auditing, the Netherlands)
Chief editor:	Jan van Bon (Inform-IT)
Editors:	Mike Pieper (Inform-IT) Axel Kolthof (Inform-IT)
Publisher:	Van Haren Publishing (info@vanharen.net)
ISBN :	978 90 8753 116 4
Editions:	First edition, first impression (IT Governance based on CobiT - a pocket guide), April 2004 Second edition, first impression, January 2007 Third edition, first impression, December 2007 Third edition, second impression, November 2009
Design & Layout:	CO2 Premedia bv, Amersfoort - NL

Acknowledgements

Publications of itSMF Netherlands are always the result of the combination of expertise and insights of many experts in the field. This Management Guide follows that tradition.

The first edition of "IT Governance based on CobiT", was reviewed by 75 experts from all over the world. By reviewing a draft Table of Contents first, this team had made sure that we created a valuable handy publication, that has been used in many countries to stimulate the awareness on CobiT.

After the Table of Contents had been agreed, the guide was written by two experts, Koen Brand and Harry Boonen. The owners and publishers of this guide wish to express their gratitude towards these two authors, who spent an enormous effort in creating the initial manuscript and processing the many review comments that contributed to this publication.

Harry Boonen is a consultant in IT Governance, business processes, business – IT alignment and outsourcing. He is a founding member of the IT Governance Network, a company specializing in IT Governance consulting and training. He has extensive experience with CobiT, and used it as an umbrella model to implement IT Governance, (business) process improvements, compliance and management of risk activities for a number of clients. Harry is past President of the ISACA Netherlands Chapter and served in ISACA boards and CACS conference committees. He is a member of the ITSMF publication board.

Koen Brand is Senior Consultant at Steenbok Adviesgroep. He has extensive experience in process improvement within IT Service Management, IT operations and systems development. He has developed and implemented practical working methods and techniques both in IT systems development and in IT Service Management, based on sound theoretical frameworks. This experience has been gathered while working for different consultancy firms at a large number of client sites around the globe.
Koen Brand is a member of the itSMF publication board, and is a black belt trainer for international delivery of the CobiT Foundations course.

The upgrade to CobiT 4.0 in 2007 didn't have significant effects on the structure of the guide, but a lot of content had to be updated, based on the revised content of CobiT 4.0. The authors again dedicated a lot of their precious time to upgrade the text, and align it to the specifications of CobiT. Their updated text on 4.0 was reviewed by a small team of reviewers that were already involved in the first edition, plus a number of experts who were known for their detailed knowledge of CobIT. The smaller upgrade to 4.1, subject to this edition, was handled as corrective maintenance, without further reviewing.

Review team 4.0 edition
- Luigi Buglione, Ph.D., École de Technologie Supérieure - ETS, Quebec, Canada
- Dr. Brian Cusack, Auckland University of Technology, New Zealand
- Ton Dohmen, Projectivate, The Netherlands
- Troy DuMoulin & Pierre Bernard, Pink Elephant International, Canada
- Han Verniers & Oscar Halfhide, LogicaCMG, The Netherlands

We wish to thank this team for their efforts in making sure the updated text aligns well to CobIT.

Review team first edition
The original review team that provided their valuable comments on the Table of Contents and on the initial manuscript, has done most of the work on the first edition. Without their extensive commenting, this guide wouldn't have been what it is now: a valuable introduction into IT Governance, based on CobIT. The owners and publishers of this book wish to express their gratitude towards this team, for their willingness to share practical insights and spend their valuable time on this project. The team was composed of 75 experts from various disciplines, and from all over the world:
- Rolf Akker, Gasunie, the Netherlands (previewer)
- Menno Arentsen, Ernst & Young EDP Audit, the Netherlands (previewer)
- Raoul Assaf, ARTUTA, Argentina
- David Aveiro, Organizational Engineering Center, Portugal
- Gustav van den Berg, UWV, the Netherlands (previewer)
- Pierre Bernard, Pink Elephant, Canada
- David Bingham, Fujitsu Consulting, UK
- Michael Böcker, Serima Consulting GmbH, Germany
- József Borda, CISA, Hunaudit Ltd., Hungary
- Maarten Bordewijk, PinkRoccade Education Services, the Netherlands
- Gerard Brantjes, Brantjes Advies Buro, the Netherlands
- Luigi Buglione, École de Technologie Supérieure (ETS) - Université du Québec, Canada
- Jeff Carter PMP, MSFmentor, USA
- Marien de Clercq, University Centre for Information Technology - University of Nijmegen, the Netherlands
- Rod Crowder, OpsCentre, Australia

- Dr Brian Cusack, Auckland University of Technology, New Zealand
- Kim Delgadillo, IBM Business Consulting Services, Belgium
- Troy DuMoulin, Pink Elephant International, Canada
- Helga Dohle, exagon consulting & solutions gmbh, Germany
- Ton Dohmen, PriceWaterhouseCoopers, the Netherlands (previewer)
- Isaac Eliahou, AtosOrigin, the Netherlands (previewer)
- Martin Erb, USA
- Péter Füzi, Salix Informatikai Bt, Hungary
- Wolfgang Goltsche, Siemens Business Services, Germany
- Vincent Haenecour, Consultis, Belgium
- Oscar Halfhide, LogicaCMG, the Netherlands
- Franz J. Hareter, Skybow AG, Switzerland
- Hussein Hassanali Haji, President ISACA - Karachi Chapter, Sidat Hyder Morshed
- Associates (Pvt.) Ltd., Pakistan
- Peter Hill, Info Sec Africa, South Africa
- Ton van den Hoogen, Tot Z BV, the Netherlands
- Göran Jonsson, Sweden
- Jörn Kettler, Serima Consulting GmbH, Germany
- Sergei Konakov, Business Experts, Russia
- Ben Kooistra, Cap Gemini Ernst & Young, the Netherlands
- Nicolay Krachun, Motorola GSG, Russia
- Emmanuel Lagouvardos, CISA, Emporiki Bank,Greece
- Alexandre Levinson, Tolkin, France
- Peiwei Lu, SinoServiceOne Ltd, P.R.China
- Steve Mann, SM2 Ltd, UK
- Luis F. Martínez, Abast Systems, Spain
- Jos Mertens, PlanIT, Belgium
- Cees Michielsen, Océ-Technologies BV, the Netherlands
- Peter Musgrave, Microsoft Ltd, UK
- Fred van Noord, GvIB Society for Information Security professionals, the Netherlands
- Peter Palatinus, Hewlett-Packard GmbH, Germany
- Michael Parkinson, KPMG, Australia
- Antonio de Pastors, Synstar Computer Services, Spain
- Vladimir Pavlov, eLine Software Inc., Ukraine
- Gert van der Pijl, Erasmus University/Eurac, the Netherlands (previewer)
- Karel van der Poel, Mirror42, the Netherlands (previewer)
- Gerrit Post, the Netherlands (previewer)
- Michael Pototsky, IT Expert, Russia

- Sylvie Prime Van Parys, CRP Henri Tudor, Luxembourg
- Ferran Puentes, Abast Systems, Spain
- Max Shanahan, Max Shanahan & Associates, Australia
- Andie Shih, ITIL International Examination Agency - North America
- Ron Sintemaartensdijk, Sogeti Nederland, the Netherlands
- Helen A. Sotiriou CISA, Emporiki Bank, Greece
- Peter Spermon RE RI CISA, Inspectie Werk & Inkomen (IWI), the Netherlands
- Rainer Sponholz, Ernst & Young AG, Germany
- Heather Stebbings MSc. DMS, CSTC Consulting, UK
- Fred Steenwinkel, VRO/IIA, the Netherlands (previewer)
- Philip Stubbs, Sheridan Insititue of Technology and Advanced Learning, Canada
- Ruedi Stucki, Zurich Financial Services, Switzerland
- Maxim Taradin, JSC Vimpelcom (Beeline™), Russia
- Karin Thelemann, Ernst & Young AG, Germany
- Sascha Thies, exagon consulting & solutions gmbh, Germany
- Antonio Valle, Abast Systems, Spain
- Wiley Vasquez, BMC Software, USA
- Han Verniers, LogicaCMG ICT Management, the Netherlands (previewer)
- Jurgen van der Vlugt, ABN AMRO Bank, the Netherlands
- Clemens Willemsen, ICTU, the Netherlands (previewer)
- Conn Wood, Foster-Melliar, South Africa

Reviewers marked with '(previewer)' are members of the core project team and contributed to the design of the guide.

As always, this kind of publications couldn't have been produced without the effort of many participants, who share the same vision: "the best way to learn is to share your vision and experience with others in the field."

Table of Contents

Foreword

This IT Governance Management Guide is the result of a project that involved many experts from all over the world. It started out as a compact reference to one framework, but it grew into an original document on IT Governance, building on many pieces of knowledge from various sources, going back into the sources of these sources, and adding pieces to the puzzle.

The project started out in the Netherlands, where a dedicated preview team designed the initial structure of this guide. In the course of the project, a huge amount of material was made available by an international team of reviewers from all kinds of origin, ranging from highly experienced practitioners in the auditing business, to presidents of ISACA chapters and academics, and to skilled IT Service Management experts and trainers. The rare combination of knowledge that was collected, enabled the development of a new instrument that will fit both worlds: Auditing and IT Service Management. It will offer the auditors a bridge to the service management business - the new wave in IT - and it will offer the service management world its long desired next step: a management instrument that enables them to put the pieces of the puzzle together, get a clear picture, and get -and remain - in control.

And that is what we're after: to be in control. Not only because new rules force us to do so, but also because it will bring some meaning to all the effort that was expanded on the way getting here. And although it definitely will not be 'the silver bullet', I do think this publication can bring us one big step ahead.

I sincerely hope you will enjoy the efforts of the team.
Any comments and suggestions regarding the content of this management guide are welcomed by the project team.

Jan van Bon
Chief editor

Contact: j.van.bon@inform-it.org

CHAPTER 1

Introduction to IT Governance & COBIT

1.1 Introduction

This book provides an overview of IT governance. IT governance is the responsibility of executives and the board of directors, and consists of the leadership, organizational structures and processes that ensure that the enterprise's IT sustains and extends the organisation's strategies and objectives.

This book has been updated to reflect the changes introduced in COBIT 4.1 and developments from other sources.

It is provided for two purposes. First, it is a quick-reference guide to IT governance for people that are not acquainted with this field of work. Second, it is a high-level introduction to ISACA's freely available framework 'COBIT' that will encourage further study. Please note that this guide follows the process structure of COBIT, since we found that to be best practice, but it differs from COBIT in several ways, adding new information to the structure, especially from the perspective of IT service management.

The management guide is aimed at business and IT (service) managers, consultants, auditors and anyone interested in learning more about the possible application of IT governance standards in the IT management domain. In addition, it provides students in IT and Business Administration with a compact reference to COBIT.

After an introduction to IT governance and COBIT in general, you will find information about ISACA's COBIT publications, since we encourage the use of COBIT. In the next section, you will find a description of the 34 processes that were identified from many international standards. This Management Guide adds new information to the various sources that were used to describe IT governance, including COBIT. Workflow diagrams and process models have been added as an extension to existing material. The last part of the book provides some guidance on COBIT implementation and the relationship with other methods and frameworks. The book can be used as an excellent companion guide to the COBIT Foundation training, or as a quick reference guide.

1.2 Context

In a book about IT governance it is sensible to analyze the position of IT governance in relation to other governance frameworks. The most comprehensive framework encountered in literature is in a discussion paper by the Chartered Institute of Management Accountants (CIMA). In this paper *enterprise governance* is a term used to describe a framework that covers both the *corporate governance* and the *business governance* aspects of the organization.

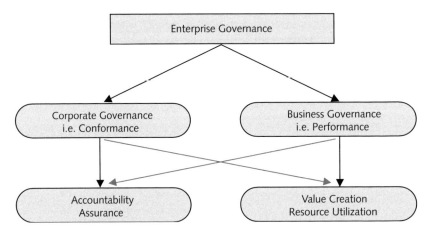

Figure 1.1 The enterprise governance framework (Source: CIMA)

CIMA uses the following definition of enterprise governance:

'Enterprise governance is the set of responsibilities and practices exercised by the board and executive management with the goal of providing strategic direction, ensuring that objectives are achieved, ascertaining that risks are managed appropriately and verifying that the enterprise's resources are used responsibly (CIMA, referencing ISACF).'

According to CIMA there are two dimensions of enterprise governance: conformance and performance. In general, the conformance dimension is approached in the retrospective view, while the performance dimension is approached in the prospective view.

The lines in figure 1.1 show that, although conformance feeds directly to accountability & assurance and performance to value creation & resource utilization, conformance can also feed to value creation & resource utilization while performance can feed to accountability & assurance.

Corporate governance, as the conformance dimension of enterprise governance, has had significant coverage following a number of well-known corporate scandals. In the wake of these scandals, which also included the demise of one of the Big Five accountancy firms, new regulations designed to strengthen corporate governance were introduced in the US, in Europe and in many other jurisdictions.
In the US the Sarbanes-Oxley Act was introduced for this reason. In Europe the Winter Report issued recommendations to provide for a modern regulatory framework for company law to the European Commission.

Among its recommendations is that companies that are traded on open markets provide a coherent and descriptive statement covering the key elements of corporate governance rules and practices in their annual report and on their web site.

The Organization of Economic Co-operation and Development (OECD) defines corporate governance in the following way:

> 'Corporate governance is the system by which business corporations are directed and controlled. The corporate governance structure specifies the distribution of rights and responsibilities among different participants in the corporation, such as the board, managers, shareholders and other stakeholders, and spells out the rules and procedures for making decisions on corporate affairs. By doing this, it also provides the structure through which the company objectives are set, and the means of attaining those objectives and monitoring performance.'

The importance of good corporate governance is recognized worldwide. It must lead to improved responsiveness to shareholder interest by attempting to balance the CEO's power with the board's ability to act as genuine custodians of the organization.

Business governance, as the performance dimension of enterprise governance, focuses on the board's role in making strategic decisions, risk assessment and understanding the drivers for business performance.

The attention to corporate governance also raises the question whether the IT used for supporting business processes is adequately controlled. This leads to an increase in attention for IT governance in many organizations. Because IT is an integral part of enterprise operations, IT governance is an integral ingredient of enterprise governance.

IT governance has been defined in many different ways. ISACA defines IT governance as follows: 'IT governance is defined as a structure of relationships and processes to direct and control the enterprise in order to achieve the enterprise's goals by adding value while balancing risk versus return over IT and its processes'

The authors of this book have defined IT governance in line with the OECD definition of corporate governance:

> IT governance is the system by which IT within enterprises is directed and controlled. The IT governance structure specifies the distribution of rights and responsibilities among different participants, such as the board, business and IT managers, and spells out the rules and procedures for making decisions on IT. By doing this, it also provides the structure through which the IT objectives are set, and the means of attaining those objectives and monitoring performance.

IT governance ensures that IT is properly aligned with business processes and is correctly organized and controlled. IT governance provides the structure that links IT processes, IT resources and information to enterprise strategies and objectives.

IT governance integrates and institutionalizes best practices of planning, organizing, acquiring, implementing, delivering, supporting, and monitoring and evaluating IT performance, to ensure that the enterprise's information and related technology support its business objectives. IT governance enables the enterprise to take full advantage of its information, thereby maximizing benefits and capitalizing on opportunities thus leveraging competitive advantage.

Table 1.1 compares the most important characteristics of corporate governance, business governance and IT governance within enterprise governance.

Corporate Governance	Business Governance	IT Governance
Separation of ownership and control	Direction and control of the business	Direction and control of IT
Retrospective	Prospective	Prospective
• Responsibilities, accountability & duties of directors/leaders • Legislative/Fiduciary compliance & control framework • Shareholder rights • Ethics & integrity • Business operations, risks & control • Financial accounting & reporting • Asset management • Risk management	• Business goals & objectives • Business strategic risk management • Business strategy & planning • Business processes & activities • Innovation & research capabilities • Knowledge & intellectual capital • Information management • Human resources management • Customer relations management • In- and external communication • Performance control	• IT objectives • Alignment with enterprise objectives • IT processes • IT resources • IT value delivery • IT performance management • Information knowledge management • IT strategy & planning • IT acquisition & implementation • IT operations, risks & control • IT asset management • IT risk management

Table 1.1 Governance characteristics

1.3 Sources for IT Governance

Regarding governance there are several sources that provide basic knowledge. In the following paragraphs some background on the major sources is presented.

COSO

In 1992, the Committee of Sponsoring Organizations of the Treadway Commission issued '*Internal Control - Integrated Framework*'. This publication established a framework for internal control and provided evaluation tools which business and other entities can use to evaluate their control systems (figure 1.2).

The framework identifies and describes five interrelated components necessary for effective internal control.

In '*Internal Control - Integrated Framework*', COSO defined internal control as a process, effected by an entity's board of directors, management and other personnel, designed to provide reasonable assurance regarding the achievement of objectives in the following categories:

- Effectiveness and efficiency of operations
- Reliability of financial reporting
- Compliance with applicable laws and regulations

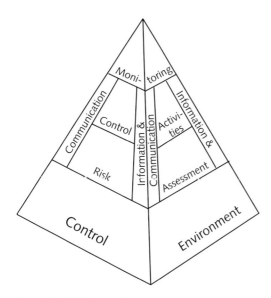

Figure 1.2 COSO Internal Control - Integrated Framework (Source COSO)

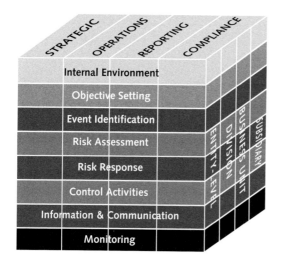

Figure 1.3 COSO Enterprise Risk Management Framework

In 2004 the COSO Enterprise Risk Management (ERM) was published. *Enterprise Risk Management* broadens internal control by expanding and elaborating a better conceptualization focusing more fully on risk.

The ERM framework expands on the internal control framework as follows:
- Four categories of objectives are specified: *Operations, reporting, compliance* and *strategic objectives*. Reporting now includes reports used internally by management and those issued to external parties. Strategic objectives have been added as a new category.
- ERM considers risk from a 'portfolio' perspective.
- The framework takes into consideration the amount of risk a company is willing to accept to achieve its goals.
- Events that can influence the company are identified. Those that can hold negative impact represent risks.
- Risk assessment is extended.
- ERM identifies four categories of risk response - *avoid, reduce, share* and *accept*. Responses are being considered both for individual risk effect and for aggregate effect.
- ERM expands on the information and communication component, considering data derived from past, present and potential future events.
- ERM describes the role and responsibilities of risk officers and expands on the role of a company's board of directors.

Code of Practice for Information Security Management (ISO/IEC 17799/BS7799, ISO 27000 series)

ISO 17799 is a code of practice for information security management. This code of practice takes a baseline approach to information security. It provides 127 information security guidelines structured under 10 major headings to enable readers to identify the security controls that are appropriate to their particular business or specific area of responsibility. The standard provides guidance on the following subjects:
- Security policy
- Security organization
- Asset classification and control
- Personnel security
- Physical and environmental security
- Communications and operations management
- Access control
- System development and maintenance
- Business continuity management
- Compliance

The ISO/IEC 17799 will be integrated as ISO 27002 into the ISO/IEC 27000-series, which has been defined by ISO for a range of information security management standards in similar fashion to the very successful ISO 9000-series quality assurance standards.

The following ISO 27000-series standards are either published or planned:
- **ISO 27000** - Vocabulary and definitions (terminology for all of these standards).
- **ISO 27001** - The Information Security Management System requirements standard (specification) against which organizations are formally certified
- **ISO 27002** - This is the Code of Practice describing a comprehensive set of information security control objectives and a menu of best-practice security controls.
- **ISO 27003** - Will be an implementation guide.
- **ISO 27004** - Will be a new Information Security Management Metrics and Measurement standard to help measure the effectiveness of information security management system implementations.
- **ISO 27005** - Will be a new Information Security Risk Management standard (will replace the recently issued BS 7799 Part 3).
- **ISO 27006** - May be a new standard containing "Guidelines for information and communications technology disaster recovery services", or may possibly be a guide to the accreditation process for certification bodies (we are awaiting further information).

ITIL

ITIL is the acronym for the 'IT Infrastructure Library' guidelines developed by the OGC in Norwich, England, for the British government. ITIL is a best practice framework for IT service management and is seen as the *de facto* global standard in this area. For example, ITIL provides the foundation for the Microsoft Operations Framework (MOF), the HP IT Service Management Reference Model, and many other proprietary frameworks.

ITIL consists of a series of books giving best practice guidance for service management, with the guidelines describing *what* rather than *how*. Service management is tailored to the size, the internal culture and the requirements of the company. An important focus is the provision of quality IT services.

In 2007 the ITIL books have been seriously revised for the second time. The well known *Service Support* book (Service Desk, Incident Management, Problem Management, Configuration Management, Change Management and Release Management) and the *Service Delivery* book (Capacity Management, Financial Management for IT Services, Availability Management, Service Level Management and IT Service Continuity Management) are replaced in this revision.

The new ITIL structure consists of five core books, giving best practice guidance; complementary material that offers support for particular market sectors or technologies and information on the web, offering topical support products, process maps and a glossary. The core ITIL books are shown in figure 1.4.

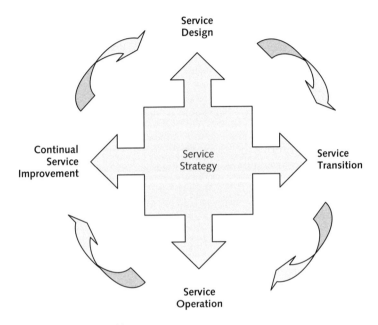

Figure 1.4 The ITIL publication structure

The books describe a service life-cycle:
- **Service Strategy** describes the overall IT service management strategy and value planning. It deals with the traditional Business-IT alignment issues and with IT governance issues. Each subsequent book in the ITIL set links to the business goals, requirements and service management principles described in this book.
- **Service Design** provides policies, architectures and documents for the planning and design of service management processes required to deliver quality services. It covers sourcing policies, and details on various processes that are required to deliver the services to the business.
- **Service Transition** provides guidance for the transition of designed services into the business environment. It combines best practices on release management,

program and risk management, to make sure that the required services are realized in Operations, and support the business.

- **Service Operation** provides guidance on how to achieve effectiveness and efficiency in the delivery and the support of quality services. It covers most of the content of the service support and service delivery guidance of ITIL v2.
- **Continual Service Improvement** provides guidance on how to identify and introduce service improvements and issues dealing with service retirement. It combines principles, practices and methods from other areas of quality management, aimed at the improved realization of initial business goals, to close the PDCA loop.

ISO/IEC 20000

At the end of 2005, the International Organization for Standardization issued a standard on IT service management. This standard was based on the BS15000 standard and is issued in two parts:

- **Part 1**: Specification for information technology service management
- **Part 2**: Code of practice for information technology service management

The specification (Part 1) defines the requirements for an organization to deliver managed services of an acceptable quality for its customers, whereas the code of practice (Part 2) provides guidance for service management processes.

When companies want to certify their quality of service provision, they can use ISO/IEC 20000. Part 1 describes the clauses a company has to adhere to in order to get the certification. Part 2 describes best practices on IT service management and can be used as a means of preparing organizations for certification.

Both the specification and the code of practice are based on a common process model, which is shown in figure 1.5.

There are 5 clusters of processes within ISO/IEC 20000 each containing one to six processes:

- **Service Delivery** includes the processes that negotiate, define and agree the actual service levels, and that report performance against targets.
- **Relationship Management** contains the processes dealing with customer and supplier, both internal and external.
- **Resolution Processes** are the closely related processes incident and problem management.
- The **Control Processes** are the core in the process model. They aim at controlling the components of service and infrastructure.

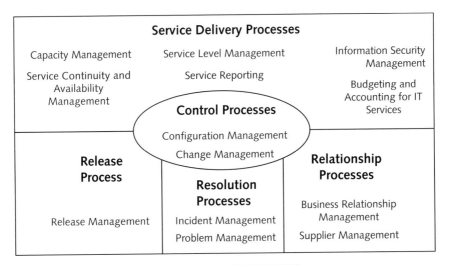

Figure 1.5 Service management processes (source: ISO/IEC 20000)

- The last cluster is called **Release Process** and contains only the release management process. Because of the strong relationship with configuration and change management, this process could have been merged with the Control Processes cluster.

CMMI / SPICE (ISO/IEC 15504)

The first Capability Maturity Model was developed by the Software Engineering Institute (SEI) of the Carnegie Mellon University and describes the principles and practices underlying software development process maturity. It was intended to help software organizations improve their software processes by following an evolutionary path from ad hoc, chaotic processes to mature, disciplined software processes. This CMM (Sw-CMM / Software CMM) was organized into five evolutive maturity levels:

0. **Initial** - The software process is characterized as ad hoc, and occasionally even chaotic. Few processes are defined, and success depends on individual effort and heroics.
1. **Repeatable** - Basic project management processes are established to track cost, schedule, and functionality. The necessary process discipline is in place to repeat earlier successes on projects with similar applications.
2. **Defined** - The software process for both management and engineering activities is documented, standardized, and integrated into a standard software process for the organization. All projects use an approved, tailored version of the organization's standard software process for developing and maintaining software.

3. **Managed** - Detailed measurements of the software process and product quality are collected. Both the software process and products are quantitatively understood and controlled.

4. **Optimizing** - Continual process improvement is enabled by quantitative feedback from the process and from piloting innovative ideas and technologies.

Predictability, effectiveness, and control of an organization's software processes are believed to improve as the organization moves up these five levels. While not rigorous, the empirical evidence to date supports this belief.

The idea of describing process maturity has expanded enormously since the first Software CMM was developed. Nowadays CMMs can be found for e.g. People, Software Acquisition, Systems Engineering, Integrated Product Development and IT Services. Several CMMs have been integrated by SEI into the Capability Maturity Model® Integration (CMMI^{SM}). CMMI is consistent and compatible with ISO/IEC 15504, which is a framework for assessment methods. This standard results from the work of the Software Process Improvement and Capability dEtermination (SPICE) initiative, which delivered a first draft in 1995.

COBIT uses a maturity model as a means of assessing the maturity of the processes described in the different COBIT domains, and to help organizations set their maturity goals for these processes. The COBIT Maturity model knows the following levels:

1. **Non-existent** - There is a complete lack of any recognizable processes. The organization has not even recognized that there is an issue to be addressed.

2. **Initial/Ad Hoc** - There is evidence that the organization has recognized that the issues exist and need to be addressed. There are, however, no standardized processes, but instead there are ad hoc approaches applied on an individual or case-by-case basis. The overall approach to management is disorganized.

3. **Repeatable but Intuitive** - Processes have developed to the stage where similar procedures are followed by different individuals undertaking the same task. There is no formal training and the communication of standard procedures and responsibilities is left to the individual. There is a high degree of reliance on the knowledge of individuals and therefore errors are likely.

4. **Defined Process** - Procedures have been standardized and documented and communicated through training. It is however left to the individual to follow these processes and it is unlikely that deviations will be detected. The procedures themselves are not sophisticated but are a formalization of existing practices.

5. **Managed and Measurable** - It is possible to monitor and measure compliance with procedures and to take action where processes appear not to be working effectively or efficiently. Processes are under improvement and provide good internal practice. Continual improvement is beginning to be addressed. Automation and tools are used in a limited and fragmented way.

6. **Optimized** - Processes have been refined to a level of external best practice, based on results of continual improvement and maturity modelling with other organizations. IT is used in an integrated way to automate the workflow, providing tools to improve quality and effectiveness and making the organization adaptive to its ever-changing environment.

Common Criteria (ISO/IEC 15408)

The Common Criteria represents the outcome of a series of efforts to develop criteria for evaluation of IT security that are broadly useful within the international community. In the 1980's and 1990's different countries worked upon developing their own criteria for security.

In June 1993, seven European and North American governmental organizations, constituting the Common Criteria project sponsoring organizations, pooled their efforts and began a joint activity to align their separate criteria into a single set of IT security criteria that could be widely used. This activity was named the Common Criteria Project. Its purpose was to resolve the conceptual and technical differences found in the source criteria and to deliver the results to ISO as a contribution to the international standard under development.

In 1999 ISO published its 'Evaluation Criteria for Information Technology Security' (ISO/IEC 15408). ISO continues the use of the term 'Common Criteria' within this document.

The Common Criteria is a means to define, assess, and measure the security aspects of IT products. The Common Criteria supports understanding of 'what the product does' (security functionality) and 'how sure you are of that' (security assurance).

The Common Criteria are useful for product developers by providing them with the knowledge they need to design IT products in such a way that they can pass an evaluation. For IT products certified against Common Criteria, customers can be sure of which security aspects of the product were tested and how these aspects were tested.

The common criteria are used to certify so called Targets of Evaluation (TOE) against criteria resulting in an evaluation assurance level for the TOE (table 1.2).

EAL1	functionally tested
EAL2	structurally tested
EAL3	methodically tested and checked
EAL4	methodically designed, tested, and reviewed
EAL5	semiformally designed and tested
EAL6	semiformally verified design and tested
EAL7	formally verified design and tested

Table 1.2 Common Criteria evaluation assurance levels

Quality Process models (Deming, BNQP, EFQM, ISO 9000)

Quality is addressed in a number of different models. Quality models aim at controlling and improving products and processes. While quality theory originates from business process environments, in many cases the ideas have also been adopted within IT.

Deming's work is very well known. He focused on process improvement in an industrial production environment as a means of improving product quality.

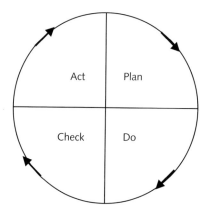

Figure 1.6 Deming cycle

Deming created a diagram (figure 1.6) to illustrate this continuous process, known as the PDCA cycle for Plan, Do, Check, Act:

• **PLAN** - Design or revise business process components to improve results.
• **DO** - Implement the plan and measure its performance.

- **CHECK** - Assess the measurements and report the results to decision makers.
- **ACT** - Decide on changes needed to improve the process.

Deming did his work on quality in the 1950's. Since that time several quality models have been developed. Some well known models will be compared here.

The *Baldrige National Quality Program (BNQP)* was started in 1987 to improve product and process quality within American organizations. Also in 1987 the *International Organization for Standardization (ISO)* issued a quality standard (ISO 9000) which was built on the specification of BS 5750. This standard has evolved into a family of ISO standards with regards to quality management. The Baldridge Model is focuses on performance, and the ISO 9000 focuses on compliance. The *EFQM Excellence Model* was introduced at the beginning of 1992 as the framework for assessing applications for the European Quality Award. It is the most widely used organizational framework in Europe and has become the basis for the majority of national and regional Quality Awards.

Each model has its own characteristics, but as shown in table 1.3, they also have many common principles.

Basic Principles of the 'Malcolm Baldridge' Model	EFQM fundamental concepts of excellence	ISO 9000 Quality Management Principles
Client-focused quality	Customer focus	Focus on your customers
Focusing on results	Results orientation	
Commitment from top management	Leadership & constancy of purpose	Provide leadership
Long-term vision of the future		
Valuation of people	People development & involvement	Involve your people
Social responsibility	Corporate social responsibility	
Management based on actions and processes	Management by processes & facts	Use a process approach
Proactive actions and rapid responses		
Continuous learning	Continuous learning, innovation & improvement	Encourage continual improvement
	Partnership development	Work with your suppliers
		Take a systems approach
		Get the facts before you decide

Table 1.3 Principles of quality models

As shown in the EFQM model (figure 1.7), quality is influenced by many factors.

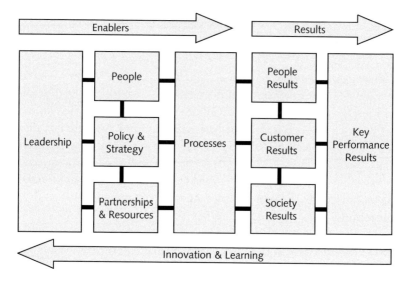

Figure 1.7 EFQM model (source EFQM)

Balanced Scorecard

The Balanced Scorecard is a management system that enables organizations to clarify their vision and strategy and translate them into action. It provides feedback about both the internal business processes and external outcomes enabling the continual improvement of strategic performance and results. Kaplan and Norton describe the importance of the balanced scorecard as follows:

'The Balanced Scorecard retains traditional financial measures. But financial measures tell the story of past events, an adequate story for industrial age companies for which investments in long-term capabilities and customer relationships were not critical for success. These financial measures are inadequate, however, for guiding and evaluating the journey that information age companies must make to create future value through investment in customers, suppliers, employees, processes, technology, and innovation.'

In their book 'The Balanced Scorecard', Kaplan and Norton set forth a hypothesis about the chain of cause and effect that leads to strategic success. There are four parts to this chain:

1. The foundation for strategic success has to do with people.
2. In a learning and growing organization the people who are involved with the business processes on a daily basis can provide ideas for improving the processes.
3. Improved business processes lead to improved products and services. The Balanced Scorecard measures customer satisfaction, which is produced by improving processes.
4. Improved customer satisfaction leads to loyal customers and increased market share.

Based on this chain of cause and effect, the balanced scorecard offers an instrument for viewing the organization from four perspectives. Metrics can be developed and data collected and analyzed for each of these perspectives (see figure 1.8).

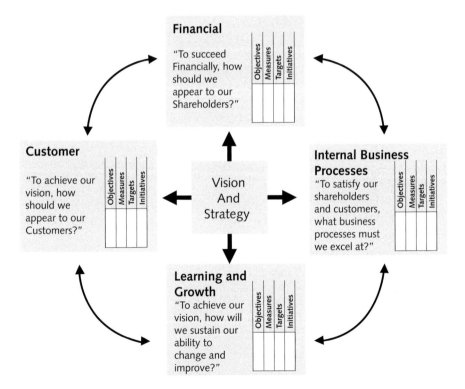

Figure 1.8 Business Balanced Scorecard (source: BalancedScorecard.org)

While the Balanced Scorecard has been developed as a business instrument, it is also used in IT.

The article *'The IT Balanced Scorecard and IT Governance'*, written by Van Grembergen, describes a cascade of balanced scorecards. He shows that a cascade of a Business Balanced Scorecard and IT Balanced Scorecards for the major IT processes can provide a measurement and management system that supports the IT governance process: defining IT strategy, developing systems and operating systems (figure 1.9). The proposed cascade of balanced scorecards fuses business and IT and in this way supports the IT governance process.

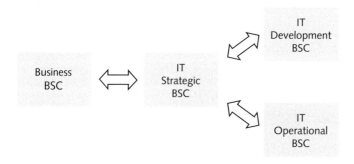

Figure 1.9 Balanced Scorecard cascade (source: Van Grembergen)

In his article Van Grembergen describes specific perspectives for IT, as depicted in the IT Balanced Scorecard (figure 1.10).
- The **User orientation** perspective represents the user evaluation of IT.
- The **Operational excellence** perspective represents the IT processes employed to develop and deliver the applications.
- The **Future orientation** perspective represents the human and technology resources needed by IT to deliver its services.
- The **Business contribution** perspective captures the business value of the IT investments.

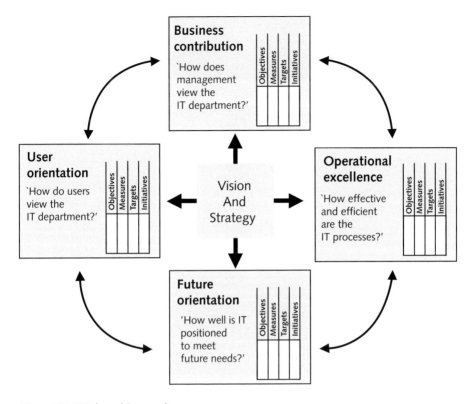

Figure 1.10 IT Balanced Scorecard

AS 8015 – 2005 – Australian Standard for Corporate Governance of IT

AS 8015 provides a framework for effective governance of the use of IT by an organization.

The Standard uses the term 'directors' to include owners, members of supervisory boards, partners, council members, senior executives, officers authorized by Acts of Parliament - in short, anyone responsible for the activities of an organization.

The framework described in AS 8015 comprises:

- a model
- guiding principles
- vocabulary

Figure 1.11 reproduces the AS 8015 model.

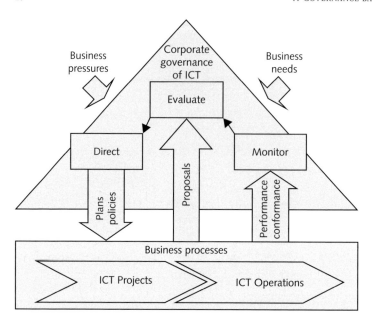

Figure 1.11 The AS 8015 model for corporate governance of IT (source: AS 8015-2005 Australian Standard for Corporate Governance of Information and Communication Technology, Standards Australia)

In the model, directors monitor and evaluate the organization's use of IT against the pressures and needs acting on it. They should then direct the development and implementation of policies and plans to address any gaps.

The Standard provides six guiding principles:
1. Establish clearly understood responsibilities for IT
2. Plan IT to best support the organization
3. Acquire IT validly
4. Ensure that IT performs well, whenever required
5. Ensure IT conforms with formal rules
6. Ensure IT respects human factors

The third component of the Standard is a vocabulary drawn from and complementing terms defined and used in the other Australian Standards for corporate governance and risk management.

In 2006, the Australian Standard was proposed to be accepted as an ISO standard, in a fast-track procedure. At the time of publishing of this management guide, no official steps were taken yet.

COBIT

COBIT stands for Control Objectives for Information and related Technology. COBIT is a model designed to control the IT function. The name of the product already betrays its auditing background. This model was originally developed by the Information Systems Audit and Control Foundation (ISACF), the research institute for the Information Systems Audit and Control Association (ISACA). In 1999 ISACF's tasks for COBIT were transferred to the IT Governance Institute (ITGI), which is an independent body within ISACA.

COBIT development started in 1994, with a first version published in 1996, and subsequent versions in 1998, 2000 and 2005. Originally, COBIT targeted auditors, end-users and management. In the current version of COBIT a clear shift is visible from a control framework toward an IT governance framework.

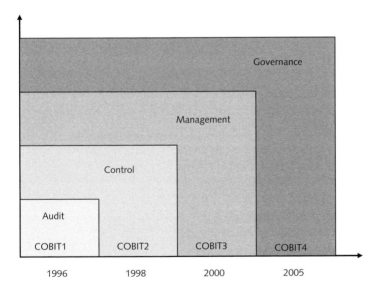

Figure 1.12 Changing emphasis of the different COBIT versions

CHAPTER 2

COBIT Background and Objectives

COBIT is a model for control of the IT environment. In developing COBIT, standards from different sources have been used, each covering a part of the information.

COBIT supports IT governance by providing a comprehensive description of the control objectives for IT processes and by offering the possibility of examining the maturity of these processes.

It helps in understanding, assessing and managing the risks together with the benefits associated with information and related IT. COBIT provides an IT governance instrument that allows managers to bridge the gap with respect to control requirements, information systems (IS) & information technology (IT) issues and business risks, in order to communicate that level of control to stakeholders. It enables the development of clear policy and good practice for the control of IT throughout organizations.

2.1 COBIT Target Groups

According to ISACA, COBIT is primarily intended for management, business users of IT and auditors. Additionally, a wide range of other disciplines, roles and functions can benefit from the guidelines provided. For instance, business and IT consultants can provide management with advice on control and governance issues and IT service management professionals can use knowledge about control objectives in order to improve their processes.

The main target groups are described in the following paragraphs.

Managers

Within organizations managers are the ones that hold executive responsibility for operation of the enterprise. They need information in order to control the internal operations and to direct business processes. IT is an integral part of business operations. COBIT can help both business and IT managers to balance risk and control investment in an often unpredictable IT environment.

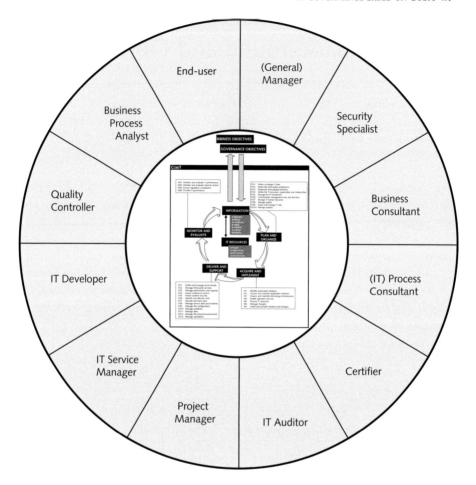

Figure 2.1 Possible target groups

End-users

Most organizations realize that having the right IT services is the responsibility of the business process owner. This is even the case when the delivery of IT services is delegated to internal or external service providers. COBIT offers a framework to obtain assurance on the security and controls of IT services provided by internal or external parties.

Auditors

In order to provide independent assurance of the quality and applicability of controls, organizations employ auditors. Often an audit committee at the board or top management

Level directs auditing. COBIT helps auditors to structure and substantiate their opinions and provide advice to management on how to improve internal controls.

Business and IT Consultants
New frameworks and methods, e.g. on IT governance often originate outside the enterprise. Business and IT consultants can bring this knowledge into the enterprise and thus provide advice to business and IT management on improving IT governance.

IT Service Management Professionals
In the IT service management community, ITIL is the dominant framework. COBIT helps to further improve IT service management by providing a framework that covers the complete lifecycle of IT systems and services.

2.2 COBIT Structure
The COBIT structure is represented by the COBIT cube, which depicts three interrelated viewpoints.

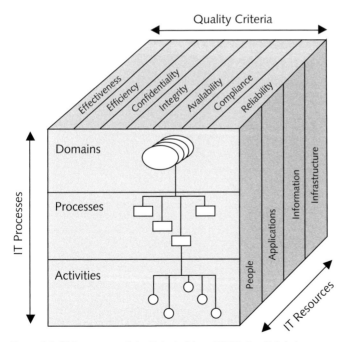

Figure 2.2 IT Governance Cube (Adapted from ISACA COBIT Cube)

Each viewpoint is described in one of the following paragraphs.

COBIT Domains and Processes

The COBIT processes have been ordered in four distinct domains, which together form a cycle. This cycle has incorrectly been compared to the Deming quality cycle, but shows a better match with the management cycle as described by Hopstaken & Kranendonk in 1988. In their original publication Hopstaken & Kranendonk presented the following four groups of processes:

- Strategy, Modelling & Planning
- Realization
- Delivery & Support
- Monitoring & Correction

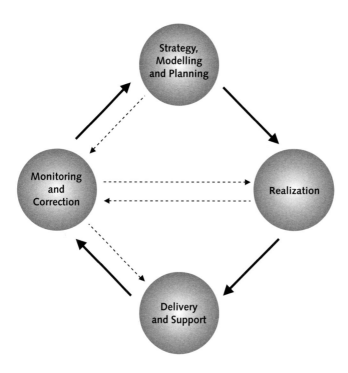

Figure 2.3 Management Cycle (Hopstaken & Kranendonk, 1988)

Strategy, Modelling & Planning provides Monitoring & Correction with the standards by which Realization and Delivery & Support can be assessed. From Monitoring there is a double-loop feedback. In the first loop Realization and Delivery & Support are provided with feedback in order to correct the process results. The second feedback-loop provides the Strategy, Modelling & Planning processes with input needed for improvement of the next cycle.

The four COBIT domains can be projected almost seamlessly onto this management cycle.

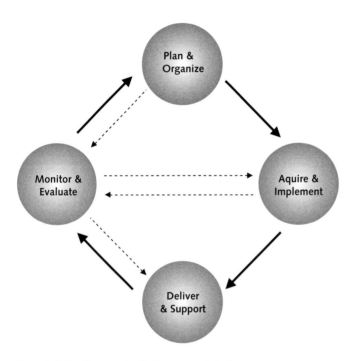

Figure 2.4 COBIT mapped onto Management Cycle

For each COBIT domain a number of processes have been identified. These are listed in the following table. Further information about the processes and activities can be found in chapter 4.

Each domain is characterised in a short description.

Plan and Organize (PO)
This domain covers strategy and tactics and is concerned with the identification of the way IT can best contribute to the achievement of business objectives. The realization

Plan and Organize (PO)		Deliver and Support (DS)	
PO1	Define a strategic IT plan	DS1	Define and manage service levels
PO2	Define the information architecture	DS2	Manage third-party services
PO3	Determine technological direction	DS3	Manage performance and capacity
PO4	Define the IT processes, organization and relationships	DS4	Ensure continuous service
		DS5	Ensure systems security
PO5	Manage the IT investment	DS6	Identify and allocate costs
PO6	Communicate management aims and direction	DS7	Educate and train users
PO7	Manage IT human resources	DS8	Manage service desk and incidents
PO8	Manage quality	DS9	Manage the configuration
PO9	Assess and manage IT risks	DS10	Manage problems
PO10	Manage projects	DS11	Manage data
		DS12	Manage the physical environment
		DS13	Manage operations
Acquire and Implement (AI)		**Monitor and Evaluate (ME)**	
AI1	Identify automated solutions	ME1	Monitor and evaluate IT performance
AI2	Acquire and maintain application software	ME2	Monitor and evaluate internal control
AI3	Acquire and maintain technology infrastructure	ME3	Ensure regulatory compliance
AI4	Enable operation and use	ME4	Provide IT governance
AI5	Procure IT resources		
AI6	Manage changes		
AI7	Install and accredit solutions and changes		

Table 2.1 Processes in the four management domains.

of the strategic vision has to be planned, communicated and managed from different points of view (e.g. information architecture and technological direction) and a proper organization and technological infrastructure must be in place.

The processes PO1 (Define a strategic IT plan), PO2 (Define the information architecture), PO3 (Determine technological direction) and PO4 (Define the IT processes, organization and relationships) make up the strategic cluster that is at the heart of the Plan and Organize domain (figure 2.5). These four processes have to be performed interactively and iteratively. Choices made in one process can influence the outcome of the other processes.

Business requirements are input to the strategic cluster, as well as the external requirements.

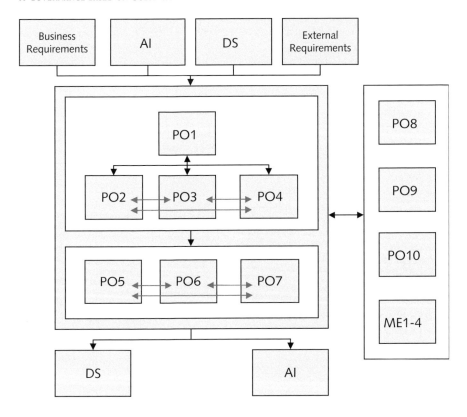

Figure 2.5 Structure Plan & Organize domain

The results of the strategic cluster are input to PO5 (Manage the IT investment), PO6 (Communicate management aims and directions) and PO7 (Manage IT human resources).

The box on the right of this figure describes PO8 (Manage quality), PO9 (Assess and manage IT risks), PO10 (Manage projects) and the ME domain. These processes have been set apart because they are a general resource to not only the processes in the Plan & Organize domain, but also to the processes in the other domains.

Acquire and Implement (AI)
In order to realize the IT goals, IT solutions need to be identified, developed or acquired, as well as implemented and integrated into the business process. In addition, to make

sure that the life cycle is continued for existing systems, this domain covers changes in and maintenance of these systems.

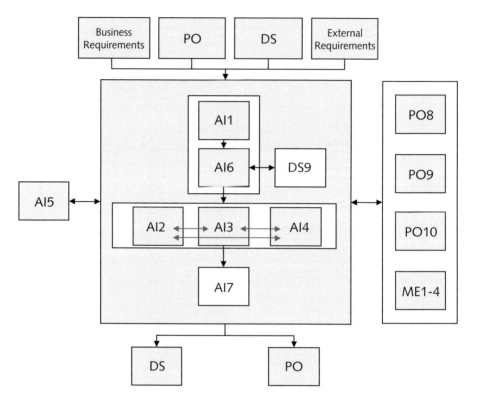

Figure 2.6 Structure Acquire & Implement domain

Based upon the information architecture and technological direction defined in the Plan & Organize domain and upon the requirements from business and external sources, process AI1 (Identify automated solutions) defines the changes needed in the IT infrastructure. AI6 (Manage changes) ensures that these changes are dealt within a responsible, controlled and non-disruptive manner. The development cluster processes AI2 (Acquire and maintain application software), AI3 (Acquire and maintain technology infrastructure) and AI4 (Enable operation and use) ensure that as a result of these processes a working information system is delivered. The process AI7 (Install and accredit solutions and changes) takes care of implementing an accredited system into the operational environment. The process AI5 (Procure IT resources) is a general resource for the other IA processes.

Because the process DS9 (Manage the configuration) has a direct relationship with AI6 (Manage changes), it has been included in the AI domain.

The box on the right of this figure describes PO8 (Manage quality), PO9 (Assess and manage IT risks), PO10 (Manage projects) and the ME domain. These processes have been set apart because they are a general resource that is also relevant for the Acquire & Implement domain.

Deliver and Support (DS)
This domain is concerned with the delivery of required services, which range from traditional operations over security and continuity aspects to training. In order to deliver services, the necessary support processes must be set up. This domain includes the processing of data by application systems, which is often classified under application controls.

The process DS1 (Define and manage service levels) is a key-process in this cluster, because it links IT Delivery & Support to the business by way of defined and agreed upon service level agreements (figure 2.7). The agreements directly influence DS2 (Manage third-party services). Both DS1 and DS2 are directly related to DS6 (Identify and allocate costs), because of the financial implications of both service level agreements and external agreements.

DS1 provides the operation cluster processes DS11 (Manage data), DS12 (Manage the physical environment) and DS13 (Manage operations) with performance criteria against which the quantity and quality of service provided will be measured.

DS8 (Manage service desk and incidents) provides a primary contact point for users with regard to any incident experienced with the operational system. DS10 (Manage problems) takes care that problems are resolved in a professional way.

Because the process DS9 (Manage the configuration) has a direct relationship with AI6 (Manage changes), it has been included in the AI domain.

Processes DS3 (Manage performance and capacity), DS4 (Ensure continuous service), DS5 (Ensure systems security) and DS7 (Educate and train users) support the other processes in this domain.

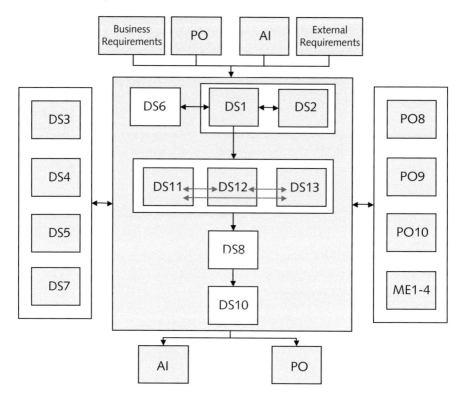

Figure 2.7 Structure Deliver & Support domain

The box on the right of this figure describes PO8 (Manage quality), PO9 (Assess and manage IT risks), PO10 (Manage projects) and the ME domain. These processes have been set apart because they are a general resource that is also relevant for the Deliver & Support domain.

Monitor and Evaluate (ME)
All IT processes need to be regularly assessed over time for their quality and compliance with control requirements. This domain addresses management supervision of the organization's control process, and independent assurance provided by internal and external audit or obtained from alternative sources.

ME1 (Monitor and evaluate IT performance) is the primary monitoring and evaluation process. It measures all processes against performance indicators (figure 2.8). It also ensures that corrective action is taken. ME2 (Monitor and evaluate internal control) monitors and evaluates for internal control objectives. ME3 (Ensure regulatory compliance) ensures that the organization complies with laws and regulations.

ME4 (Provide IT governance) provides for proper IT governance within the organization.

The box on the right of this figure describes PO8 (Manage quality), PO9 (Assess and manage IT risks) and PO10 (Manage projects). These processes have been set apart because they are a general resource that is also relevant for the Monitor & Evaluate domain.

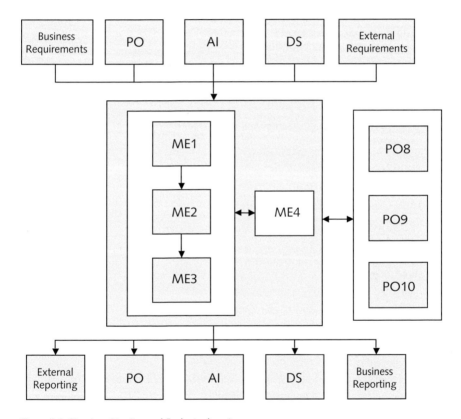

Figure 2.8 Structure Monitor and Evaluate domain

IT Resources

COBIT identifies four classes of IT resources:

1. **People** - The human resources needed to plan, organize, acquire, deliver, support, monitor and evaluate information systems and services.
2. **Applications** - The automated user systems and manual procedures that process the information.
3. **Information** - Data as input and output of information systems, in any form used by the business.
4. **Infrastructure** - Technology and facilities that enable the processing of applications.

Quality Criteria

An underpinning concept for COBIT is that control of IT is approached by looking at the information that is needed to support the business requirements. In establishing the criteria for information, COBIT analyzed existing and known reference models:

- Quality requirements:
  - Quality
  - Cost
  - Delivery
- Fiduciary requirements (COSO report):
  - Effectiveness and efficiency of operations
  - Reliability of information
  - Compliance with laws and regulations
- Security requirements:
  - Confidentiality
  - Integrity
  - Availability

The effectiveness criterion covers the Quality requirement. The delivery aspect of quality overlaps the availability aspect of security requirements and also effectiveness and efficiency. Finally, the cost aspect of quality is also covered by efficiency.

For the fiduciary requirements, ISACA used COSO's well-accepted definitions for effectiveness and efficiency of operations, reliability of information and compliance with laws and regulations, rather than attempting new definitions. However, reliability of information was expanded to include all information - not just financial information.

With respect to the security requirements, COBIT identified confidentiality, integrity and availability as the key elements - these same three elements, it was found, are used worldwide in describing IT security requirements.

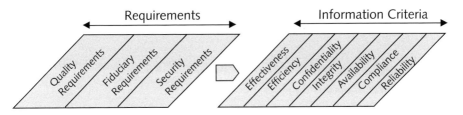

Figure 2.9 Transition from requirements to quality criteria

For information, a number of quality criteria are identified. COBIT also refers to these as Information Criteria. For this management guide, the quality criteria are defined as follows:

- **Effectiveness** - The extent to which the information serves the defined objectives.
- **Efficiency** - The extent to which activities with regard to the provision of information are carried out at an acceptable cost and effort.
- **Confidentiality** - The extent to which data is only accessible to a well-defined group of authorized persons.
- **Integrity** - The extent to which data corresponds with the actual situation represented by that data.
- **Availability** - The extent to which a system or service is available to the intended users at the required times.
- **Compliance** - The extent to which processes act in accordance with those laws, regulations and contractual arrangements to which the process is subject.
- **Reliability of information** - The extent to which appropriate information is provided for management to operate the entity and to exercise its financial and compliance reporting responsibilities.

COBIT describes the information criteria in a somewhat different way:
- **Effectiveness** deals with information being relevant and pertinent to the business process as well as being delivered in a timely, correct, consistent and usable manner.
- **Efficiency** concerns the provision of information through the optimal (most productive and economical) use of resources.
- **Confidentiality** concerns the protection of sensitive information from unauthorized disclosure.
- **Integrity** relates to the accuracy and completeness of information as well as to its validity in accordance with business values and expectation.
- **Availability** relates to information being available when required by the business process now and in the future. It also concerns the safeguarding of necessary resources and associated capabilities.

- **Compliance** deals with complying with those laws, regulations and contractual arrangements to which the business process is subject; i.e., externally imposed business criteria as well as internal policies.
- **Reliability of information** relates to the provision of appropriate information for management to operate the entity and for management to exercise its fiduciary and governance responsibilities.

The business process owners define what information is needed in order to meet their business objectives. COBIT, as an instrument for governing the IT environment, identifies the processes within the four domains required to meet the quality criteria relevant to the business, using the necessary IT resources.

The overall COBIT structure is depicted in figure 2.10, which also shows its relationship with business objectives.

2.3   COBIT as an IT Governance Framework

COBIT as a Control Framework

COBIT focuses on enterprise governance and the need to improve controls in organizations. COBIT provides a framework to control IT and supports the following five requirements for an IT control framework:
- Providing a sharper business focus
- Ensuring a process orientation
- Having a general acceptability among organizations
- Defining a common language
- Helping to meet regulatory requirements

Business Focus
To provide the information that the enterprise requires to achieve its objectives, the enterprise needs to manage and control IT resources using a structured set of processes to deliver the required information services.
- COBIT achieves sharper business focus by aligning IT with business objectives.
- The measurement of IT performance should focus on IT's contribution to enabling and extending the business.
- COBIT supported by appropriate business-focused metrics can be used to ensure that the primary focus is service delivery and not technical proficiency.

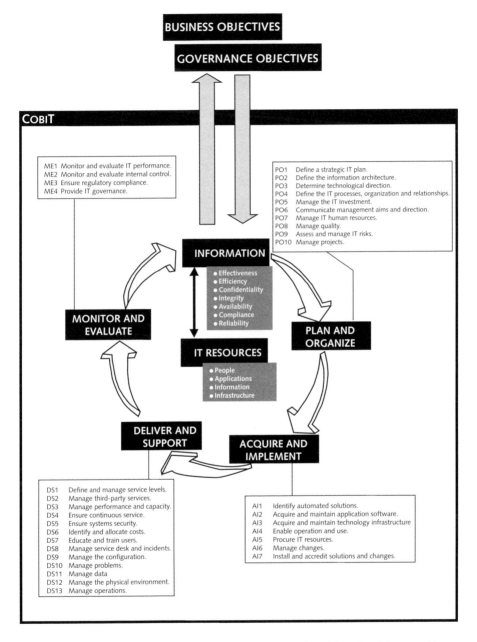

Figure 2.10 COBIT IT Processes defined within the four domains (adapted from COBIT Framework)

Process Orientation

This ensures that activities are organized into processes that are owned based on identified responsibilities. Let's consider an example of updating the website of a company. The website's content is deemed published by the company and has legal liabilities for the company. Therefore, a process needs to be designed and somebody needs to approve the changes. This is referred to as change management.

When organizations implement COBIT, their focus becomes more process-orientated.

Incidents and problems no longer divert attention from the process.

Exceptions can be clearly defined as part of the standard processes.

The processes define, describe and assign roles and responsibilities and enable the organization to maintain control while dealing with exceptional circumstances.

General Acceptability

A control framework comprises globally accepted best practices. Best practices evolve over time by including inputs from experienced people in the industry. Over several implementation cycles the practices become proven. These best practices are formalized as a framework.

- COBIT is a proven and globally accepted standard for increasing the contribution of IT to organizational success.
- The framework continues to improve and develop to keep pace with the best practices.
- IT professionals from all over the world contribute their ideas and time to regular review meetings.

Regulatory Requirements

Regulatory compliance is often an expensive and onerous task. It is easier to demonstrate compliance if the control framework is based on accepted standards. Auditors will also find it easier to review controls when an accepted model is adopted.

- Recent corporate scandals have increased regulatory pressures on Boards of Directors to report their status and ensure that internal controls are appropriate. This covers IT controls as well.
- Organizations constantly need to improve IT performance and demonstrate adequate controls over their IT activities.
- Many IT managers, advisors, and auditors are turning to COBIT as the de facto response to regulatory IT requirements.

Common Language

Over time, best practices tend to acquire distinctive terminology that is defined by a framework. Common terminology enables communication within the organization, among peers in other companies, and with external parties/third parties or consultants.

In today's world of cross-functional teams, task forces are often headed by people who are not aware of the size of the implementation because their expertise lies in another area of the organization. Coordination within and across project teams and organizations can play a key role in the success of any project.
A framework helps get everybody on the same page by defining critical terms and providing a glossary.

Principles of IT Governance
The board of directors and the executive management are responsible for IT governance. IT involves structures and processes that direct the organization toward achieving its objectives. According to ITGI, IT governance is based on four principles:
- Direct and control
- Responsibility
- Accountability
- IT Activities

Direct and Control
'*Direct and control*' are the two key concepts of IT governance:
- **Direct** - The Director provides direction to implement a change. To provide effective direction, the Director needs to understand the intended change. The Director directs another person to bring about the change
- **Control** - Control ensures that the objective is achieved and no undesired incidents occur.

Responsibility
The CEO is ultimately responsible for internal control. Senior managers assign responsibility for the establishment of specific internal control policies and procedures to personnel responsible for the unit's functions. Internal control is the responsibility of everyone in an organization and should be an explicit or implicit part of the job description.

Accountability
Accountability is the obligation of employees to account for, report on, or explain their actions about the use of resources entrusted to them. Management is accountable to the board of directors, which provides governance, guidance, and supervision. It is essential for individuals to know how their actions contribute to the achievement of the

objectives. The control environment is influenced by the extent individuals recognize that they may be held accountable.

IT Activities
IT activities are effective when there is good IT governance.

IT Governance Focus Areas

The IT governance focus areas describe the topics that executive management needs to address to govern IT within their enterprises. COBIT provides a generic process model that represents all the processes normally found in IT functions. The COBIT process model has been mapped to the IT governance focus areas. This provides a link between operational execution of processes and governance of IT.

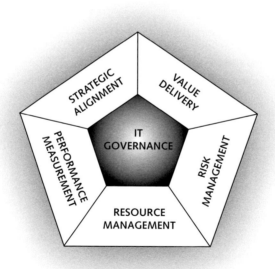

Figure 2.11 Focus areas used within COBIT

The following focus areas are included by ITGI in COBIT 4.1 to describe the focus of the COBIT processes:

Strategic Alignment focuses on ensuring the linkage of business and IT plans; on defining, maintaining and validating the IT value proposition; and on aligning IT operations with enterprise operations.

Value Delivery is about executing the value proposition throughout the delivery cycle, ensuring that IT delivers the promised benefits against the strategy, concentrating on optimizing costs and proving the intrinsic value of IT.

Risk Management requires risk awareness by senior corporate officers, a clear understanding of the enterprise's appetite for risk, understanding of compliance requirements, transparency about the significant risks to the enterprise, and embedding of risk management responsibilities into the organization.

Resource Management is about the optimal investment in, and the proper management of, critical IT resources: people, applications, information, and infrastructure. Key issues relate to the optimization of knowledge and infrastructure.

Performance Measurement tracks and monitors strategy implementation, project completion, resource usage, process performance and service delivery, using, for example, balanced scorecards that translate strategy into action to achieve goals measurable beyond conventional accounting.

CHAPTER 3

COBIT and Related IT Governance Publications

COBIT (Control Objectives for Information and related Technology is organized in three levels (see figure 3.1) to support:
- Executive management and boards
- Business and IT management
- Governance, assurance, control and security professionals

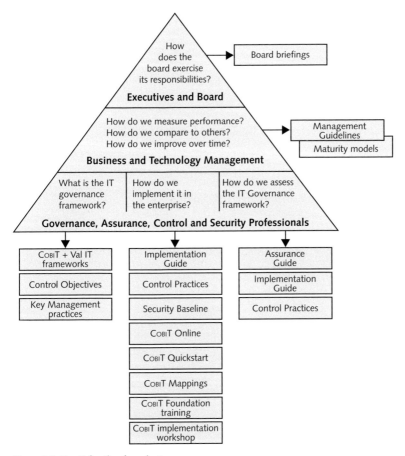

Figure 3.1 COBIT family of products

This figure suggests that management guidelines, control objectives, maturity models and framework are separate publications. As of COBIT 4.0 these publications have been included in the main COBIT publication.

Primarily of interest for executives are:
- Board Briefing on IT Governance 2nd edition
- Information Security Governance: Guidance to Board of Directors and Executive Management 2nd Edition
- Enterprise Value: Governance of IT Investments (Val IT), covering:
  - The Val IT Framework
  - The Business Case
  - The ING Case Study

Primarily of interest to business and technology management is:
- Management Guidelines

Primarily of interest to governance, assurance, control and security professionals are:
- Framework
- Control Objectives
- COBIT Control Practices: Guidance to Achieve Control Objectives for Successful IT Governance, 2nd Edition
- IT Assurance Guide
- IT Assurance Framework (ITAF)
- IT Control Objectives for Sarbanes-Oxley 2nd edition
- IT Control Objectives for Basel II
- IT Governance Implementation Guide Using COBIT ® and Val IT™, 2nd edition
- COBIT Security Baseline: An Information Security Survival Kit, 2nd Edition
- COBIT Online
- COBIT Quickstart
- COBIT Mapping
- COBIT Foundation Course

Further are special books developed for students to make them aware of IT Governance structures of COBIT:
- COBIT in Academia

Other publications are the IT Governance Domain Practices and Competencies Series:
- IT Alignment: Who Is in Charge
- Optimizing Value Creation From IT investments
- Information Risks: Whose Business Are They?
- Governance of Outsourcing
- Measuring and Demonstrating the Value of IT

COBIT is a living framework. At this moment there are several projects working on different aspects of COBIT. Information on new developments can always be found on the ISACA web site.

All publications can be downloaded from the ISACA (www.isaca.org) and IT Governance Institute (www.itgi.org) web sites. Download of COBIT 4.1, the IT Governance Implementation Guide, the IT Assurance Guide, the COBIT Security Baseline and the COBIT mappings with other standards is restricted to ISACA members. The COBIT Control Practices can only be bought in the ISACA Bookstore.
On these websites you can also find information on training options.
For an overview of all research within ISACA and the ITGI you can go to the ISACA website: all current projects are listed under Research.
The next paragraphs briefly describe COBIT and related IT governance publications.

3.1 COBIT 4.1

This book covers the COBIT Framework, the Control Objectives and the Management Guidelines topics. In this publication there is build the logical relationship between Business goals and IT goals, Process goals and Activity goals supported by Metrics as Outcome Measures and Performance Indicators. Therefore the relation between enterprise governance and IT governance is clear.

The framework is built on the following principle: to provide the information the enterprise requires to achieve its objectives, the enterprise needs to manage and control IT resources using a structures set of processes to deliver the required information services. The COBIT framework delivers tools to support alignment to the business requirements.

The framework describes the high-level control objectives for each process within the COBIT domains. By addressing these objectives, the business process owner can ensure that the IT environment is adequately controlled.

Figure 3.2 shows, by IT process and domain, which information criteria are impacted by the high-level control objectives. It further indicates which IT resources and IT governance focus areas are applicable. The IT governance focus areas, information criteria and IT resources have been explained earlier in this chapter.

Process	IT Governance Focus Areas					COBIT Resources				COBIT Information Criteria						
	Strategic Alignment	Value Delivery	Resource Management	Risk Management	Performance Measurement	People	Application	Information	Infrastructure	Effectiveness	Efficiency	Confidentiality	Integrity	Availability	Compliance	Reliability
Plan and Organize																
PO1 Define a strategic IT plan.	P		P	S		✓	✓	✓	✓	P	S					
PO2 Define the information architecture.	P	S	P	S			✓	✓		S	P	S	P			
PO3 Determine technological direction.	S	S	P	S				✓	✓	P	P					
PO4 Define the IT processes, organization and relationships.	S		P	P		✓				P	P					
PO5 Manage the IT Investment.	S	S	S		S	✓	✓		✓	P	P					S
PO6 Communicate management aims and Direction.	P			P		✓		✓		P					S	
PO7 Manage IT human resources.	P		P	S	S	✓				P	P					
PO8 Manage quality.	P	S		S		✓	✓	✓	✓	P	P		S			S
PO9 Assess and manage IT risks.	P			S		✓	✓	✓	✓	S	S	P	P	P	S	S
PO10 Manage projects.	P	S	S	S	S	✓	✓		✓	P	P					
Acquire and Implement																
AI1 Identify automated solutions.	P	P	S	S			✓		✓	P	S					
AI2 Acquire and maintain application software.	P	P		S			✓			P	P		S			S
AI3 Acquire and maintain technology infrastructure.			P						✓	S	P		S	S		
AI4 Enable operation and use.	S	P	S	S		✓	✓		✓	P	P		S	S	S	S
AI5 Procure IT resources.		S	P			✓	✓	✓	✓	S	P				S	
AI6 Manage changes.		P	S			✓	✓	✓	✓	P	P		P	P		S
AI7 Install and accredit solutions and changes.	S	P	S	S	S	✓	✓	✓	✓	P	S		S	S		
Deliver and Support																
DS1 Define and manage service levels.	P	P	P		P	✓	✓	✓	✓	P	P	S	S	S	S	S
DS2 Manage third-party services.		P	S	P	S	✓	✓	✓	✓	P	P	S	S	S	S	S
DS3 Manage performance and capacity.	S	S	P	S	S		✓		✓	P	P			S		
DS4 Ensure continuous service.	S	P	P	P	S	✓	✓	✓	✓	P	S			P		
DS5 Ensure systems security.				P		✓	✓	✓	✓			P	P	S	S	S
DS6 Identify and allocate costs.			S	P		S	✓	✓	✓	✓		P				P
DS7 Educate and train users.	S	P		S		✓				P	S					
DS8 Manage service desk and incidents.	S	P			S	✓	✓			P	P					
DS9 Manage the configuration.			P	S			✓	✓	✓	P	S			S		S
DS10 Manage problems.			P	S		✓	✓	✓	✓	P	P			S		
DS11 Manage data.		P	P					✓				P				P
DS12 Manage the physical environment.			S	P					✓	P	P					
DS13 Manage Operations.			P			✓		✓	✓	P	P		S	S		
Monitor and Evaluate																
ME1 Monitor and evaluate IT performance.					P	✓	✓	✓	✓	P	P	S	S	S	S	S
ME2 Monitor and evaluate internal control.		P		P		✓	✓	✓	✓	P	P	S	S	S	S	S
ME3 Ensure regulatory compliance.	P			P		✓	✓	✓	✓						P	S
ME4 Provide IT governance.	P	P	P	P	P	✓	✓	✓	✓	P	P	S	S	S	S	S

Figure 3.2 Control Objectives Summary Table (adapted from COBIT)

When looking at control objectives for processes and applicable IT governance focus areas and information criteria, not all will satisfy the different business requirements for information to the same degree:

- **Primary (P)** - The defined control objective directly impacts the IT governance focus area or information criteria concerned.
- **Secondary (S)** - The defined control objective satisfies only to a lesser extent the IT governance focus area or information criteria concerned.
- **Blank** - When not indicated as primarily or secondary, requirements for the IT governance focus area or information criteria could be applicable or not at all.

Not all control objectives will necessarily impact the different IT resources to the same degree. Therefore, COBIT indicates the applicability of the IT resources that are specifically managed by the process under consideration (not those that merely take part of the process). Organizations should carefully examine these control objectives to review which ones are most applicable for their own specific situation.

The COBIT control objectives show the control objectives for each process in more detail. Over 200 detailed control objectives are described to provide control measures for each process. The number of detailed control objectives for each process varies from four to fifteen.

The management guidelines cover for each process the process inputs and outputs, a RACI (Responsible, Accountable, Consulted and/or Informed) chart, the process goals and metrics, and the maturity model.

3.2 COBIT Control Practices: Guidance to Achieve Control Objectives for Successful IT Governance, 2nd Edition

The Control practice statements are aligned with COBIT 4.1 and are a supplement to COBIT. They are meant to expand the capabilities of COBIT by providing the practitioner with an additional level of detail, based on good practices. The current IT processes, business information requirements and detailed control objectives define what needs to be done to implement an effective control structure, to avoid risks and to gain value of the implementation of control objectives. The control practices provide a more detailed how, why and what, needed by management, service providers, end users and control professionals to implement justified and designed specific controls. The COBIT conceptual framework is thus extended with more specific implementation focus. The control practices are also referred to in the IT Assurance Guide and the IT Governance Implementation Guide.

3.3 IT Assurance Guide

The IT Assurance guide is an update of the Audit Guidelines[1]. This book uses the term 'assurance' consistently, as it is broader than the term 'audit'. Assurance also covers evaluation activities not governed by internal and/or external audit standards.

The assurance guide enables the review of IT processes against recommended detailed control objectives to provide management assurance and/or advice for improvement. It provides guidance on how to use COBIT to support a variety of IT assurance activities and for preparing assurance plans that are integrated with the COBIT Framework and Control Objectives.

Using the IT Assurance guide helps the auditors to underpin their conclusions, because COBIT is based on authoritative criteria from standards and good/best practices from private and public standard creation bodies.

While explaining what the IT Assurance guide covers, it is prudent to indicate their limitations:

1. The IT Assurance Guide is not intended as a tool for creating an overall audit plan. Such a plan considers factors like including past weaknesses, risks to the organization, known incidents, new developments and strategic choices.
2. The IT Assurance Guide is not intended as a tool for teaching auditing, even though they incorporate the generally accepted basics of (IT) auditing.
3. The IT Assurance Guide does not attempt to explain in detail how computerized planning, assessment, analysis and documentation tools can be used to support and automate the audit of IT processes.
4. The IT Assurance Guide is neither exhaustive nor definitive, but will evolve together with COBIT.

The IT Assurance roadmap described in the IT Assurance guide consists of three stages (see figure 3.3):

*   **Planning** - resulting in an (annual) IT Assurance plan
*   **Scoping** - resulting in detailed scope and objectives for the assurance initiative
*   **Executing** - resulting in the assurance conclusion

---

1   The IT Assurance Guide is planned to be published early 2007.

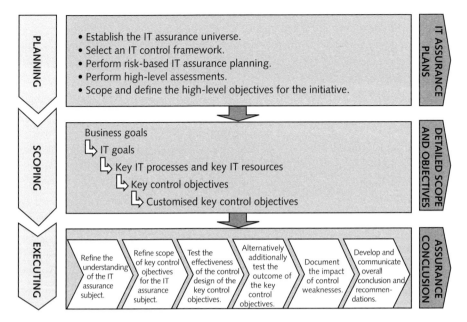

Figure 3.3 IT Assurance Roadmap (Source: IT Assurance Guide)

The steps in the execution roadmap are described in more detail, in the following.

The first step is refining an understanding of the environment in which the assurance will be performed. This implies understanding the organization to select the correct assurance scope and objectives. The assurance scope and objectives will be communicated to and agreed upon by all stakeholders.

The second step is refining the scope and is determined by selecting a subset of the assurance universe (i.e. process, system, or application) on one hand and a set of controls to be reviewed on the other hand, by:

• Analyzing business and IT goals
• Selecting processes and controls
• Analyzing the inherent risk of material control objectives not being met and the amount of assurance review and testing required
• Finalizing scope

In the third step the control design will be tested:

• Evaluate the design of the controls
• Confirm that controls are 'placed in operation'

- Assess the operational effectiveness of the control
- The assurance professional must determine whether:
    - Documented control processes exist
    - Appropriate evidence of control processes exists
    - Responsibility and accountability are clear and effective
    - Compensating controls exist, where necessary

In the fourth step the outcome or effectiveness of the control is tested. To do that, the assurance professional looks for direct and indirect evidence of the control's impact on the quality of the process output. This implies the direct and indirect substantiation of measurable contribution of the control to the IT process and activity goals, recording direct and indirect evidence of actually achieving the outcomes, as documented in CobiT.

In the fifth step, when control weaknesses are found, they have to be properly analysed, based on the severity of the observed weaknesses and the risk for business impact they may have.

In the final step, the assurance professional documents any identified control weaknesses and resulting threats and vulnerabilities, and identifies and documents the actual and potential impact, e.g. through root-cause analysis. Conclusions and recommendations are formulated and communicated to the responsible party for further steps and remedial actions.

3.4   IT Assurance Framework

The IT Assurance Framework (ITAF) has to provide guidance on the design, conduct and report on IT audit and assurance assignments. It also defines terms and concepts specific to IT assurance and promulgates standards dealing with assurance professional roles and responsibilities, skills and diligence, conduct, and reporting requirements. ITAF addresses three categories of standards: general, performance and reporting. It is envisioned that ITAF will not only be a document for the profession, it will also guide the ISACA Standards Board in the fulfillment of its charge: development of guidance for the IS assurance profession. After reviewing and incorporating comments/issues raised from the exposure process, the final version of the document is scheduled to be released in the fourth quarter of 2007.

3.5 IT Control Objectives for Sarbanes-Oxley 2nd edition

The second edition is published in draft in April 2006 and is released in Autumn 2006. Events as ENRON, Worldcom, and others have forced a new era in the history of business, characterized by a firm resolve to increase corporate responsibility. The Sarbanes-Oxley Act of 2002 was created to restore investor confidence in US public markets, which were devastated by business scandals and lapses in corporate governance. Despite all the publicity surrounding the Sarbanes-Oxley Act of 2002, relatively little attention has focused specifically on the role of information technology (IT) in the financial reporting process. This is unfortunate, given that the accuracy and timeliness of financial reporting is, at most companies, heavily dependent on a well-controlled IT environment.

Many of the IT professionals being held accountable for the quality and integrity of information generated by their IT systems are not well versed in the objectives of internal control, which is critical when dealing with the requirements of Sarbanes-Oxley. This is not to suggest that risk is not being managed by IT, but rather that it may not be formalized or structured in a way required by an organization's management or its auditors.

In cooperation with contributors, the IT Governance Institute has designed the book 'IT Control Objectives for Sarbanes-Oxley'. It serves primarily as a reference for executive management and IT control professionals, including IT management and assurance professionals, when evaluating an organization's IT controls required by the US Sarbanes-Oxley Act of 2002.

3.6 IT Control Objectives for Basel II

IT Control Objectives for Basel II provides a framework for managing information risk in the context of Basel II. This document addresses two target groups: IT practitioners and financial services experts. In applying the framework presented in this publication, financial services organizations are able to apply recognized processes and controls to the information technology space. The IT control objectives and management processes outlined, address the role of Information Technology in operational risk, and the resulting tasks for IT practitioners, internal IT auditors, IT risk managers and information security officers. This publication is planned for the end of 2007.

3.7   IT Governance Implementation Guide Using CoBIT® and Val IT™, 2nd edition

The objective of this guide is to provide readers with a methodology for implementing or improving IT governance using CoBIT® and Val IT™. It will support the reader's role whether it relates to management, compliance, risk, value, performance, security or assurance of IT.

The implementation guide delivers a roadmap for implementing IT governance using CoBIT and Val IT (in 15 steps), covering the following:
- **Identify Needs** - Raise awareness and obtain management commitment, define scope, define risks, define resources and deliverables and plan program.
- **Envision Solution** - Assess actual performance, define target for improvement and analyze gaps and identify improvements.
- **Plan Solution** - Define projects and develop improvement plan.
- **Implement Solution** - Implement the improvements, monitor implementation performance and review program effectiveness.
- **Operationalize Solution** - Build sustainability and identify new governance requirements.

The Primary focus of Val IT processes is on delivering business value by:
- **Value Governance** - Establishing a broad governance, monitoring and control framework that delivers a clear and active linkage between the enterprise strategy and the portfolio of IT-enabled investment programmes that execute the strategy.
- **Portfolio Management** - Managing the overall portfolio to optimize value to the enterprise
- **Investment Management -** Managing the results of individual investment programmes, including business, process, people, technology and organizational change enabled by the business and by IT projects that make up the programmes.

For more detailed information about Val IT view the following ITGI publications:
Enterprise Value: Governance of IT Investments (Val IT), covering:
- The Val IT Framework
- The Business Case
- The ING Case Study

The guide is supported by the IT Governance Implementation Guide – Toolkit, covering several tools for implementing successful IT Governance. This toolkit can be downloaded from the IT Governance Institute website (www.itgi.org).
Target groups for this publication are:

- Board and Executive
- Business Management
- IT Management
- IT Audit
- Risk and compliance.

3.8   COBIT Quickstart™ 2nd Edition

COBIT, in its complete form, can be a bit overwhelming for those who operate with a small IT staff and who may not have the resources to implement all of COBIT. This version of COBIT is a subset of the entire volume. Only those control objectives that are considered the most critical are included, so that the implementation of COBIT 's fundamental principles can go easily, effectively and relatively quickly.

This special version of COBIT is a baseline for the small to medium enterprises (SMEs), or companies that don't want to implement all COBIT processes. It is a good starting point for other enterprises to move to an appropriate level of control and governance of IT. This publication is based on the strategic nature of IT to the business and contains a developed self-assessment form to review exceptions. This publication was developed in response to comments that COBIT, in its complete form, can be a bit overwhelming. Those who operate with a small IT staff often do not have the resources to implement COBIT completely. This version of COBIT constitutes a subset of the entire COBIT volume. Only those control objectives that are considered the most critical are included, so that the implementation of COBIT's fundamental principles can take place easily, effectively and relatively quickly. A CD-ROM is included. This updated publication is available in October 2007.This special version of COBIT is a baseline for small or medium enterprises (SMEs) and other organizations where IT is not mission-critical or essential for survival. It can also serve as a starting point for other enterprises in their move towards an appropriate level of control and governance of IT. A new edition is planned for 2007.

3.9   COBIT Online

COBIT Online is designed as a web-based service and available to anyone with an Internet connection. It makes COBIT more accessible and user-friendly. By using My COBIT, you can construct and download your own, personalized version of COBIT for your own use.

Whether you are a current user of COBIT or planning to adopt COBIT as the preferred framework for IT governance, COBIT Online provides easy and rapid access to all of the COBIT resources. With COBIT Online, you can browse and search best practices, download customized guidance, perform benchmarking and more.

Benchmarking in COBIT Online allows you to evaluate and input your enterprise's scores and then extract comparisons with other users.
COBIT Online evolves based on user feedback and is regularly updated.

Access options and associated capabilities:
- **Baseline** (nonmembers and nonsubscribers) - The baseline capability includes the ability to download PDFs (e.g. COBIT 4.0) and access the discussion area. There is no charge; however, a user online account must exist or be created.
- **Basic subscriber** (member benefit) - ISACA members have the ability to browse all of COBIT (minus the Control Practices and *Quickstart* entries), download PDFs (COBIT 4.1 IT Governance *Implementation Guide and IT Assurance Guide*), secure access to survey results, and access the discussion area.
- **Full subscriber + benchmarking** - This provides full benchmarking capability in addition to the ability to browse all of COBIT (including Control Practices pertaining to all control objectives and *Quickstart* entries), download PDFs, access the discussion area and search and create My COBIT. For the annual subscription fees see: www.isaca.org/COBITonline/.

3.10 COBIT Security Baseline: An Information Security Survival Kit, 2nd Edition

This guide, based on COBIT 4.1, consists of a comprehensive set of resources that contains the information organizations need to adopt an IT governance and control framework. COBIT covers security in addition to all the other risks that can occur with the use of IT. COBIT Security Baseline focuses on the specific risk of IT security in a way that is simple to follow and implement for the home user or the user in small to medium enterprises, as well as executives and board members of larger organizations. It provides the following elements:
- Useful background reading:
  - An introduction to information security—what it means and what it covers
  - An explanation of why security is important and examples of the most common things that can go wrong
  - Thought-provoking questions to help determine risks

- The COBIT -based security baseline, providing key controls
- In addition to the mapping against COBIT 4.1, a mapping against the updated ISO / IEC 17799:2005 information security standard and presented as ISO / IEC 27002:2007
- Information security survival kits, providing essential awareness messages for:
  - Home users
  - Professional users
  - Managers
  - Executives
  - Senior executives
  - Boards of directors / trustees
- An appendix containing a summary of technical security risks

3.11 CoBiT Mappings

Currently a number of mappings between COBIT and other generally accepted standards have been developed, as described below. Extra mappings are planned for autumn 2007 and for 2008. They will be mapped against COBIT 4.1 and the available mappings are planned to be remapped.

- Aligning COBIT, ITIL and ISO 17799 for Business Benefit. This mapping is published in November 2005 and based on COBIT 3.0. The mapping gives a good and practical overview of the matching of the different COBIT processes and control objectives with the standards ITIL and ISO 17799. It can be downloaded from the IT Governance Institute website (www.itgi.org).
- COBIT Mapping: Mapping ISO/IEC 17799:2005 With COBIT 4.0. This mapping is published in December 2006 and only downloadable for ISACA members. The mapping is detailed and based on COBIT 4.0. It is very useful for people working in the security environment, who should invest in what is common between COBIT and ISO 17799:2005. It can be downloaded from the IT Governance Institute website (www.itgi.org).
- COBIT Mapping overview of international IT Guidance, 2nd Edition (May 2006). This mapping is a global mapping of COBIT with 13 other internationally accepted standards. These standards are:
  - COSO (Internal Control - Integrated Framework)
  - ITIL (IT Infrastructure Library books Software Asset Management, Service Support, Service Delivery, Planning to Implement Service Management, ICT Infrastructure Management, Application Management, Security Management and Business Perspective I)
  - ISO/IEC 17799:2005 (Code of Practice for Information Security Management)

- FIPS PUB 200 (US standard for Minimum Security Requirements for Federal Information and Information Systems)
- ISO/IEC TR 13335 (Information Technology - Guidelines for the Management of IT Security, technical report)
- ISO/IEC 15408:2005 / Common Criteria / ITSEC (Security Techniques - Evaluation Criteria for IT Security is based on the Common Criteria for Information Technology Security Evaluation 2.0)
- PRINCE2 (Project management based on Managing Successful Projects with PRINCE2)
- PMBOK (A guide to the Project Management Body of Knowledge, an American standard for project management)
- TickIT (A scheme for assessment and certification of an organization's software quality management system)
- CMMI (Capability Maturity Model Integration)
- TOGAF 8.1 (Open Group Architecture Framework is a detailed method and set of supporting tools for developing an enterprise architecture)
- IT Baseline Protection Manual (Handbook recommending standard security safeguards for typical IT systems from German BSI) and
- NIST 800-14 (Publication Generally Accepted Principles and Practices for Securing Information Technology Systems, an American standard). It can be downloaded from the IT Governance Institute website (www.itgi.org).
- COBIT Mapping: Mapping PMBOK to COBIT 4.0 (August 2006). This detailed mapping is downloadable for ISACA members.
- COBIT Mapping: Mapping SEI's CMM for Software to COBIT 4.0 (August 2006). This detailed mapping is downloadable for ISACA members.
- COBIT Mapping: Mapping of CMMI for Development V1.2 With COBIT 4.0 (March 2007). This detailed mapping is downloadable for ISACA members.
- COBIT Mapping: Mapping PRINCE2 with COBIT (January 2007). This detailed mapping is downloadable for ISACA members.
- COBIT Mapping: Mapping ITIL v2 with COBIT 4.0 (January 2007). This detailed mapping is downloadable for ISACA members.
- COBIT Mapping: Mapping of TOGAF 8.1 with COBIT 4.0 (June 2007). This detailed mapping is downloadable for ISACA members.
- A number of extra mappings, e.g. between ITIL v3 and COBIT 4.1 is planned for 2008.

3.12 COBIT Foundation Course™ and Exam

Organizations using COBIT benefit from the development of COBIT competences among their key professionals. COBIT training courses help professionals master COBIT and utilize this knowledge for effective implementation within their organizations. Sustainable COBIT competences helps IT organizations and departments align with the business goals and objectives, and generate strategic value from IT.

With the growing adoption of COBIT, ISACA recognized the need for structured and formal education and worked together with ITpreneurs™ to develop authentic COBIT learning solutions. The COBIT curriculum comprises the following courses:

- COBIT Awareness Course (2 hours, self paced e-learning)
- COBIT Foundation Course (8 hours, self paced e-learning)
- COBIT Foundation Exam (1 hour, online 40 questions)
- COBIT for Sarbanes Oxley (5 hours, self paced e-learning)
- COBIT Foundation Classroom training (2 days)
- COBIT Foundation Classroom training including COBIT game (2 ½ days)
- COBIT Implementation Course (2 days)
- Based on this work also Pink Elephant now provides 3 day instructor-led course titled COBIT Foundation

3.13 Board Briefing on IT Governance 2nd Edition

Addressed to boards of directors, supervisory boards, audit committees, chief executive officers, chief information officers and other executive management, Board Briefing on IT Governance is based on COBIT. It explains why IT governance is important, what the issues are and what boards' and executives' responsibility is for managing them. The document covers:

- A summarized background on governance
- Where IT governance fits in the larger context of enterprise governance
- A simple framework with which to think about IT governance
- Questions board members should ask
- Good practices as well as critical success factors
- Performance measures board members can track
- A maturity model against which to benchmark the organization

3.14 Information Security Governance: Guidance to Board of Directors and Executive Management 2nd Edition

To achieve effectiveness and sustainability in today's complex, interconnected world, information security must be addressed at the highest levels of the organization, not regarded as a technical specialty relegated to the IT department.

Organizations today face a global revolution in governance that directly affects their information management practices. Following the high-profile organizational failures of the past decade, legislatures, statutory authorities and regulators have created a complex array of new laws designed to force improvement in organizational governance, security, controls and transparency. Coupled with previous laws in these areas and information retention and privacy, these new laws and regulations, together with significant threats of information system disruptions from hackers, worm, virus perpetrators and terrorists create an unprecedented need for a governance approach to information management.

Information Security Governance: Guidance for Boards of Directors and Executive Management, first published in 2002, has been updated to reflect the changes in the environment, and to include many ideas and outcomes of those organizations that embrace good Information Security Governance.

This guide covers such issues as:
• What is information security governance?
• Why is information security important?
• Who should be concerned with information security governance?
• What should information security governance deliver?
• What can be done to successfully implement information security governance?

3.15 Val IT, A new framework and supporting publications addressing the governance of IT-enabled business investments

Val IT is a governance framework that consists of a set of guiding principles, and a number of processes conforming to those principles that are further defined as a set of key management practices.

The Val IT framework will be supported by publications and operational tools and provides guidance to:
• Define the relationship between IT and the business and those functions in the organization with governance responsibilities.

- Manage an organization's portfolio of IT-enabled business investments.
- Maximize the quality of business cases for IT-enabled business investments with particular emphasis on the definition of key financial indicators, the quantification of 'soft' benefits and the comprehensive appraisal of the downside risk.

Val IT addresses assumptions, costs, risks and outcomes related to a balanced portfolio of IT-enabled business investments. It also provides benchmarking capability and allows enterprises to exchange experiences on best practices for value management.'
- Val IT Framework
- Val IT Business Case
- Val IT ING Case Study

The Val IT publications are largely based upon the ideas set forward in John Thorp's book: 'The Information Paradox: Realizing the Business Benefits of Information Technology'.

3.16 COBIT in Academia

COBIT in Academia is a set of educational materials that professors and teachers can use to explain and present COBIT in their curricula and courses of information systems management, information security management, information systems auditing and/or accounting information systems. This educational package was constructed using the advice and counsel of a global group of academics and practitioners. The purpose was to create a more focused approach for teaching and presenting COBIT in the classroom.

COBIT in Academia is available to all professors who pledge to share their own COBIT teaching materials.
The set includes the following material:
- Student Book
- PowerPoint Presentation
- Case Study
- Caselets

COBIT in Academia is available to academics by completing a brief questionnaire.

3.17 IT Governance Domain Practices and Competencies Series

In chapter 2 the IT governance focus areas have been described. Based upon these focus area's a number of separate publications have been issued. These can be downloaded by ISACA members from the ISACA and ITGI websites. The publications are sold as books in the ISACA bookstore.

IT Alignment: Who Is in Charge

For any enterprise to achieve long-term sustainable success, it is essential that employees in all elements that comprise the enterprise, fully understand corporate objectives and work together in a properly controlled and coordinated way to ensure that those objectives are met.

Optimizing Value Creation From IT investments

Successful acquisition and deployment of IT often require significant allocation of resources and should therefore be subject to the same initial scrutiny and 'before and after' monitoring as any other type of investment. No investment, IT included, should be undertaken without full knowledge of the expected cost and anticipated return, as related to risk. High-risk projects have a higher likelihood of failure, so to compensate for those that fail, high-risk projects should carry a higher return expectation.

Information Risks: Whose Business Are They?

The management of risks is a cornerstone of IT governance, ensuring that the strategic objectives of the business are not jeopardized by IT failures. Risks associated with technology issues are increasingly evident on board agendas, as the impact on the business of an IT failure can have devastating consequences. Risk is, however, as much about failing to grasp an opportunity to use IT - for example, to improve competitive advantage or operating efficiency - as it is about doing something badly or incorrectly.

Governance of Outsourcing

Outsourcing of some or all of the services within larger companies is seen as a way to contain, if not diminish, costs and simultaneously increase control over revenue utilization. The increasing costs arise, to a substantial extent, from the difficulty of retaining internal technical expertise in a 24x7x365 global, dynamic market. A strategic organizational response is to disaggregate the value chain and push the service provision out to third parties.

Measuring and Demonstrating the Value of IT

Measuring IT performance should be a key concern of business and IT executives as it demonstrates the effectiveness and added business value of IT. Many methods, tools and best practices exist to support these executives with the performance management responsibilities. Traditional performance methods as return on investment (ROI) capture the financial worth of IT projects and systems, but reflect only a limited (tangible) part of the value that can be delivered by IT. There also exist methods to measure the value of IT for the business such as IT Balanced Scorecard. All practices for measuring the value of IT should be combined with good portfolio management, which helps to generate an optimal mix of projects, creates a solid foundation for a balanced IT governance approach in the organization.

CHAPTER 4

COBIT Process Descriptions

4.1 Introduction

A powerful and central theme in COBIT is the focus on IT processes and controls. In the COBIT 4.1 publication the following core components for each of the 34 IT processes are described in more detail:

- A process description summarizing the process objectives, with the high-level control objective represented in a waterfall. This page also shows the mapping of this process to the information criteria, IT resources and IT governance focus areas by way of P to indicate primary relationship and S to indicate secondary.
- The detailed control objectives for this process.
- The process inputs and outputs, activities & RACI chart, goals and metrics.
- The maturity model for the process.

The inputs, outputs, responsibilities, metrics and goals are illustrative but not prescriptive or exhaustive. They provide a basis of expert knowledge from which each enterprise should select what efficiently and effectively applies to it based on enterprise strategy, goals and policies.

In this IT Governance Management Guide all processes were described briefly. The ISACA publication 'COBIT 4.1' describes each process in more detail. COBIT 4.1 shows a vast improvement over previous versions in bringing information about processes together.

For each process this Management Guide includes a description of the Goal, Activities, Inputs and Outputs and Relationships with other processes. For each process a workflow diagram is provided. In this workflow diagram the activities are clustered into meaningful steps.

Diagrams on the relationships with other processes have been developed as well.

4.2 PO Plan and Organize

PO1 Define a Strategic IT Plan

Goal

To define a strategic IT plan to manage and direct all IT resources in line with the business strategy and priorities.

Activities

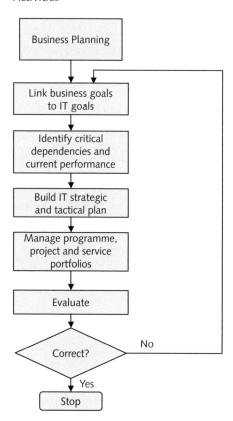

Figure 4.1 Activities of 'Define a strategic IT plan'

The following activities are carried out in the IT process 'Define a strategic IT plan':
- Link business goals to IT goals
- Identify critical dependencies and current performance
- Build an IT strategic plan
- Build IT tactical plans
- Analyze program portfolios and manage project and service portfolios

Relationships with other processes

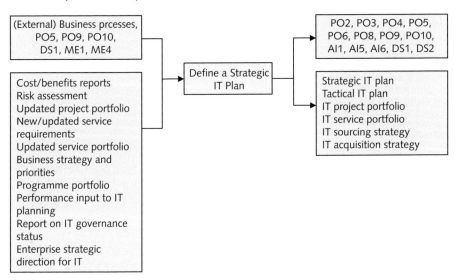

Figure 4.2 Relationships of 'Define a strategic IT plan'

PO2   Define the Information Architecture

Goal

To create and regularly update a business information model and define the appropriate systems to optimize the use of the information.

Activities

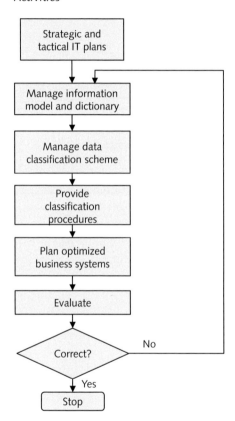

Figure 4.3 Activities of 'Define the information architecture'

The following activities are carried out in the IT process 'Define the information architecture':

- Create and maintain a corporate/enterprise information model
- Create and maintain corporate data dictionary(ies)
- Establish and maintain data classification scheme
- Provide data owners with procedures and tools for classifying information systems
- Utilize the information model, data dictionary and classification scheme to plan optimized business systems

Relationships with other processes

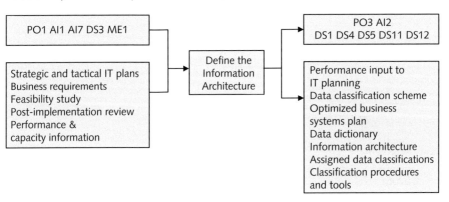

Figure 4.4 Relationships of 'Define the information architecture'

PO3   Determine Technological Direction
Goal
To determine the technology direction which supports the business strategy and goals.

Activities

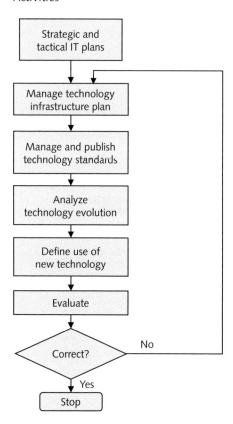

Figure 4.5 Activities of 'Determine technological direction'

The following activities are carried out in the IT process 'Determine technological direction':
- Create and maintain a technology infrastructure plan
- Create and maintain technology standards
- Publish technology standards
- Monitor technology evolution
- Define (future)(strategic) use of new technology

Relationships with other processes

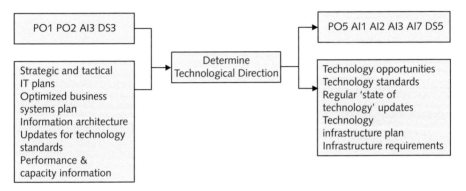

Figure 4.6 Relationships of 'Determine technological direction'

PO4   Define the IT Processes, Organization and Relationships
Goal
To define an IT organization considering requirements for staff, skills, functions, accountability, authority, roles, responsibilities, and supervision. This organization is to be embedded into an IT process framework.

Activities

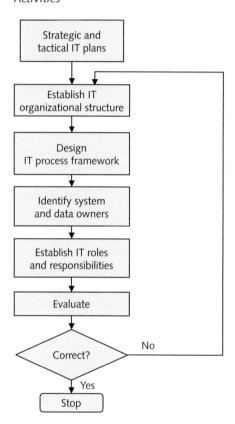

Figure 4.7 Activities of 'Define the IT Processes, organization and relationships'

The following activities are carried out in the IT process 'Define the IT processes, organization and relationships':

- Establish IT organizational structure, including committees and linkages to the stakeholders and vendors
- Design an IT process framework
- Identify system owners
- Identify data owners
- Establish and implement IT roles and responsibilities, including supervision and segregation of duties

Relationships with other processes

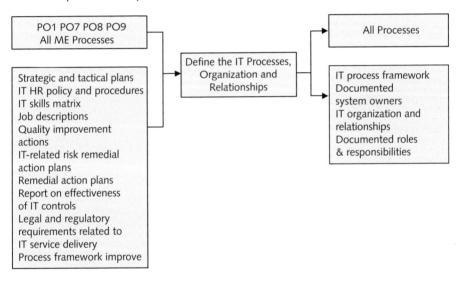

Figure 4.8 Relationships 'Define the IT Processes, organization and relationships'

PO5   Manage the IT Investment
Goal
To establish and maintain a framework to manage IT-enabled investment programs.

Activities

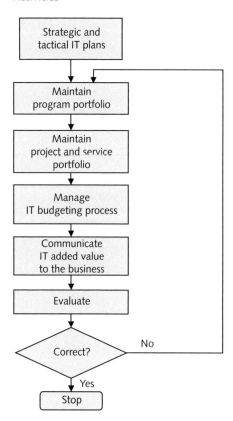

Figure 4.9 Activities of 'Manage the IT investment'

The following activities are carried out in the IT process 'Manage the IT investment':
- Maintain the program portfolio
- Maintain the project portfolio
- Maintain the service portfolio
- Establish and maintain the IT budgeting process
- Identify, communicate and monitor IT investment, cost and value to the business

Relationships with other processes

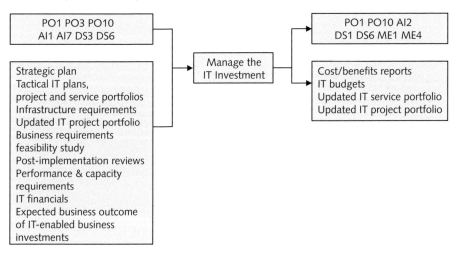

Figure 4.10 Relationships of 'Manage the IT investment'

PO6   Communicate Management Aims and Direction
Goal

To communicate management aims and direction by developing an enterprise IT control framework, and defining and communicating policies.

Activities

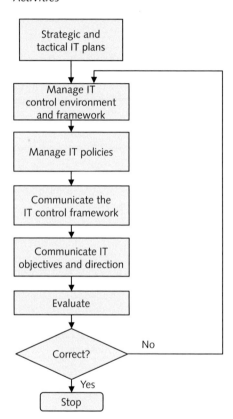

Figure 4.11 Activities of 'Communicate management aims and direction'

The following activities are carried out in the IT process 'Communicate management aims and direction':
- Establish and maintain an IT control environment and framework
- Develop and maintain IT policies
- Communicate the IT control framework and IT objectives and direction

Relationships with other processes

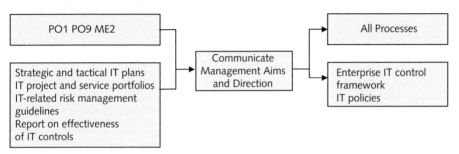

Figure 4.12 Relationships of 'Communicate management aims and direction'

PO7   Manage IT Human Resources

Goal

To manage IT human resources by acquiring, maintaining and motivating a competent workforce for the creation and the delivery of IT services to the business.

Activities

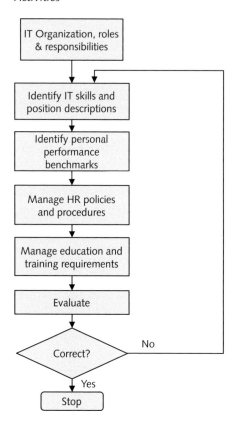

Figure 4.13 Activities of 'Manage IT human resources'

The following activities are carried out in the IT process 'Manage IT human resources':
- Identify IT skills, position descriptions, salary ranges and personal performance benchmarks
- Execute HR policies and procedures relevant to IT (recruit, hire, evaluate, compensate, train, appraise, promote and dismiss)

Relationships with other processes

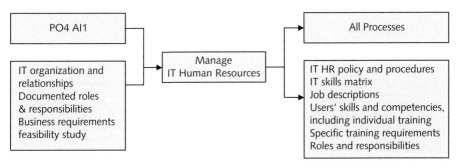

Figure 4.14 Relationships of 'Manage IT human resources'

PO8   Manage Quality

Goal

To manage quality by developing and maintaining a quality management system, which includes proven development and acquisition processes and standards.

Activities

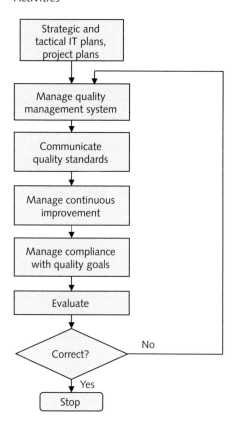

Figure 4.15 Activities of 'Manage quality'

The following activities are carried out in the IT process 'Manage quality':
- Define a quality management system
- Establish and maintain a quality management system
- Build and communicate quality standards through the organization
- Build and manage the quality plan for continual improvement
- Measure, monitor and review compliance with the quality goals

Relationships with other processes

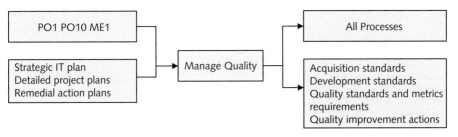

Figure 4.16 Relationships of 'Manage quality'

PO9   Assess and Manage IT Risks

Goal

To assess and manage IT risks by creating and maintaining a risk management framework.

Activities

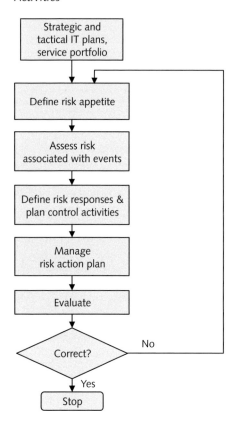

Figure 4.17 Activities of 'Assess and manage IT risks'

The following activities are carried out in the IT process 'Assess and manage IT risks':
- Determine risk management alignment (e.g., assess risk)
- Understand relevant strategic business objectives
- Understand relevant business process objectives
- Identify internal IT objectives and establish risk context
- Identify events associated with objectives
- Assess risk associated with events
- Evaluate risk responses
- Priorities and plan control activities
- Approve and ensure funding for risk action plans
- Maintain and monitor a risk action plan

Relationships with other processes

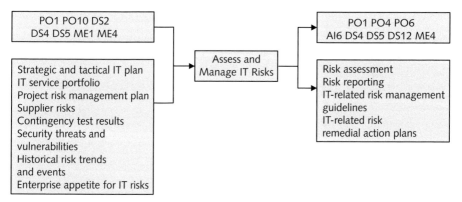

Figure 4.18 Relationships of 'Assess and manage IT risks'

PO10 Manage Projects

Goal

To manage projects by establishing a program and project management framework for the management of all IT projects.

Activities

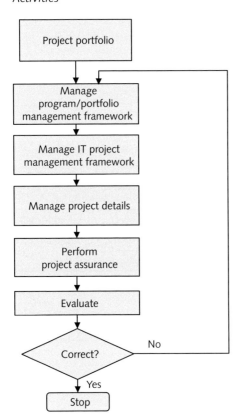

Figure 4.19 Activities of 'Manage projects'

The following activities are carried out in the IT process 'Manage projects':
- Define a program/portfolio management framework for IT investments
- Establish and maintain an IT project management framework
- Establish and maintain an IT project monitoring, measurement and management system
- Build project charters, schedules, quality plans, budgets, and communication and risk management plans
- Assure the participation and commitment of project stakeholders
- Assure the effective control of projects and project changes
- Define and implement project assurance and review methods

Relationships with other processes

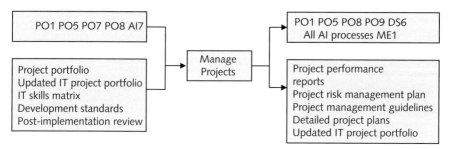

Figure 4.20 Relationships of 'Manage projects'

4.3   AI   Acquire and Implement

AI1   Identify Automated Solutions
Goal
To analyze the need for new applications or functions, before acquisition or creation, and to ensure business requirements are satisfied in an effective and efficient approach.

Activities

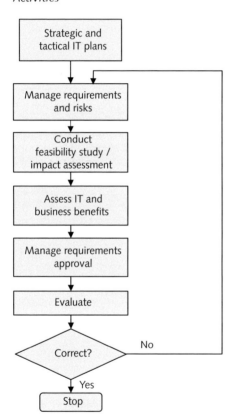

Figure 4.21 Activities of 'Identify automated solutions'

The following activities are carried out in the IT process 'Identify automated solutions':
- Define business functional and technical requirements
- Establish processes for integrity / currency of requirements
- Identify, document and analyze business process risk
- Conduct a feasibility study / impact assessment in respect of implementing proposed business requirements
- Assess IT operational benefits of proposed solutions
- Assess business benefits of proposed solutions
- Develop a requirements approval process
- Approve and sign off on solutions proposed

Relationships with other processes

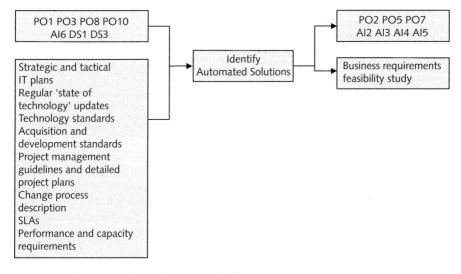

Figure 4.22 Relationships of 'Identify automated solutions'

AI2   Acquire and Maintain Application Software

Goal

To acquire and maintain application software in line with business requirements.

Activities

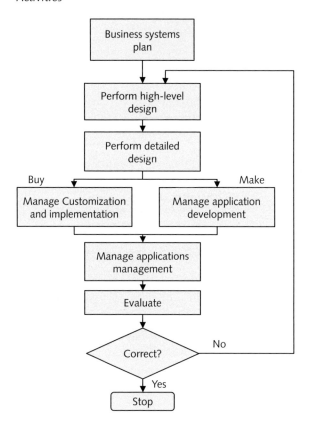

Figure 4.23 Activities of 'Acquire and maintain application software'

The following activities are carried out in the IT process 'Acquire and maintain application software':

- Translate business requirements into high-level design specification
- Prepare detailed design and technical software application requirements
- Specify application controls within the design
- Customize and implement acquired automated functionality
- Develop formalized methodologies and processes to manage the application development process
- Create a software quality assurance plan for the project
- Track and manage application requirements
- Develop a plan for the maintenance of software applications

Relationships with other processes

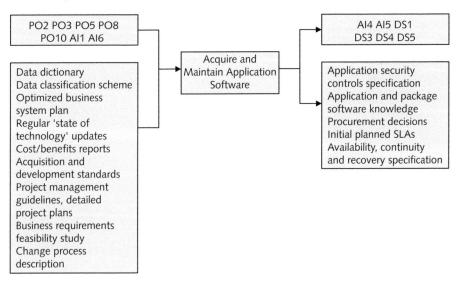

Figure 4.24 Relationships of 'Acquire and maintain application software'

AI3   Acquire and Maintain Technology Infrastructure
Goal
To acquire and maintain a technology infrastructure in line with the business needs and business applications.

Activities

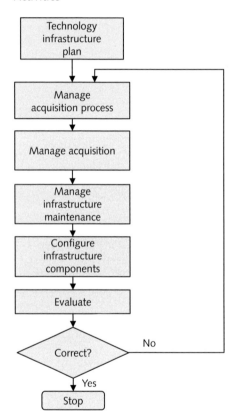

Figure 4.25 Activities of 'Acquire and maintain technology infrastructure'

The following activities are carried out in the IT process 'Acquire and maintain technology infrastructure':
* Define an acquisition procedure / process
* Negotiate acquisition and acquire the required infrastructure with (approved) vendors
* Define a strategy and maintenance plan for infrastructure
* Configure infrastructure components

Relationships with other processes

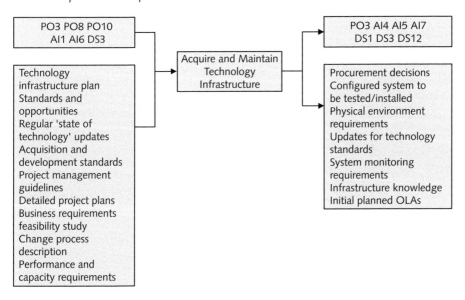

Figure 4.26 Relationships of 'Acquire and maintain technology infrastructure'

AI4   Enable Operation and Use

Goal

To ensure a proper use and operations of applications and infrastructure by providing documentation and training.

Activities

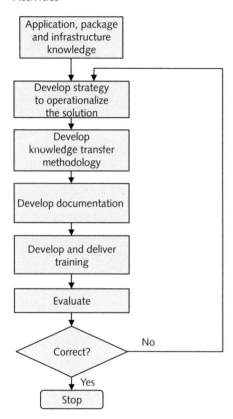

Figure 4.27 Activities of 'Enable operation and use'

The following activities are carried out in the IT process 'Enable operation and use':
- Develop a strategy to operationalize the solution
- Develop a knowledge transfer methodology
- Develop end-user procedure manuals
- Develop technical support documentation for operations and support staff
- Develop and deliver training
- Evaluate training results and enhance documentation as required

Relationships with other processes

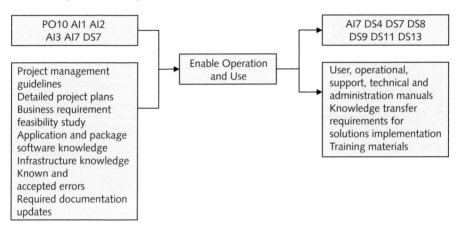

Figure 4.28 Relationships of 'Enable operation and use'

AI5   Procure IT resources
Goal
To procure the IT resources people, applications, information and infrastructure.

Activities

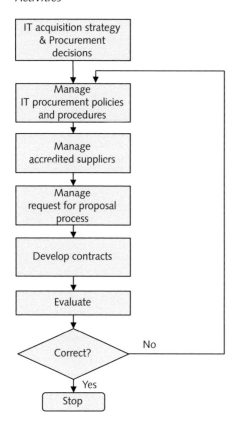

Figure 4.29 Activities of 'Procure IT resources'

The following activities are carried out in the IT process 'Procure IT resources':
- Develop IT procurement policies and procedures aligned with procurement policies at the corporate level
- Establish/maintain a list of accredited suppliers
- Evaluate and select suppliers through a request for proposal (RFP) process
- Develop contracts that protect the organization's interests
- Procure in compliance with established procedures

Relationships with other processes

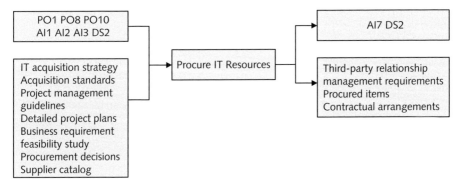

Figure 4.30 Relationships of 'Procure IT resources'

AI6   Manage Changes

Goal

To manage all changes relating to infrastructure and applications in a controlled manner.

Activities

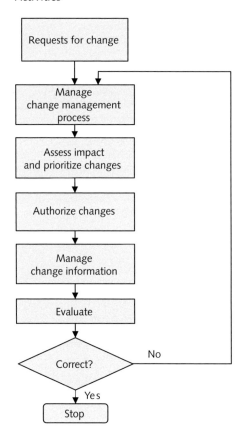

Figure 4.31 Activities of 'Manage changes'

The following activities are carried out in the IT process 'Manage changes':
- Develop and implement a process to consistently record, assess and prioritize change requests
- Assess impact and prioritize changes based on business needs
- Assure that any emergency change and critical change follows the approved process
- Authorize changes
- Manage and disseminate relevant information regarding changes

Relationships with other processes

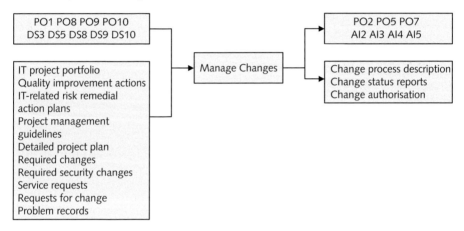

Figure 4.32 Relationships of 'Manage changes'

AI7   Install and Accredit Solutions and Changes

Goal

To install and accredit new operational systems in line with the agreed expectations and outcomes.

Activities

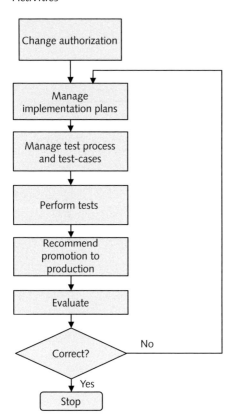

Figure 4.33 Activities of 'Install and accredit solutions and changes'

The following activities are carried out in the IT process 'Install and accredit solutions and changes':
- Build and review implementation plans
- Define and review a test strategy (entry and exit criteria) and an operational test plan methodology
- Build and maintain a business and technical requirements repository and test cases for accredited systems
- Perform system conversion and integration tests on test environment
- Deploy test environment and conduct final acceptance tests
- Recommend promotion to production based on agreed accreditation criteria

Relationships with other processes

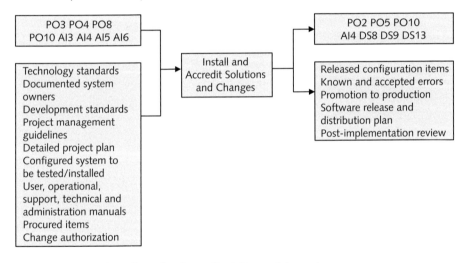

Figure 4.34 Relationships of 'Install and accredit solutions and changes'

4.4 DS   Deliver and Support

DS1   Define and Manage Service Levels
Goal
To define and manage service levels to enable alignment between IT services and the related business requirements.

Activities

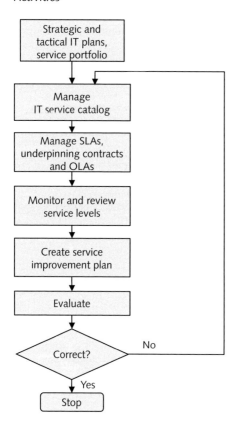

Figure 4.35 Activities of 'Define and manage service levels'.

The following activities are carried out in the IT process 'Define and manage service levels':
- Create a framework for defining IT services
- Build an IT service catalog
- Define service level agreements (SLAs) for critical IT services
- Define operating level agreements (OLAs) for meeting SLAs
- Monitor and report end-to-end service level performance
- Review SLAs and underpinning contracts
- Review and update IT service catalog
- Create service improvement plan

Relationships with other processes

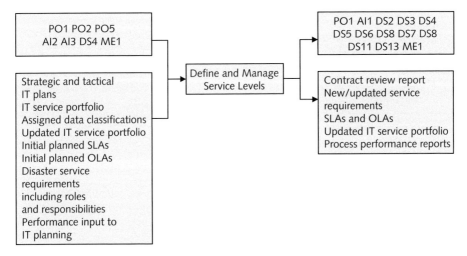

Figure 4.36 Relationships of 'Define and manage service levels'

DS2   Manage Third-party Services

Goal

To manage the services provided by third-parties to meet the business requirements with minimized risks.

Activities

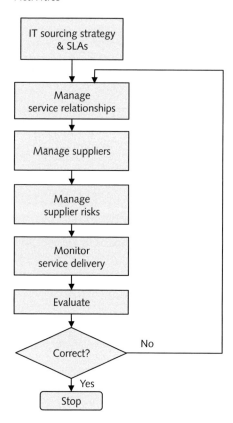

Figure 4.37 Activities of 'Manage third-party services'

The following activities are carried out in the IT process 'Manage third-party services':
- Identify and categorize third-party service relationships
- Define and document supplier management processes
- Establish supplier evaluation and selection policies and procedures
- Identify, assess, report and mitigate supplier risks
- Monitor supplier service delivery
- Evaluate long-term goals of the service relationship for all stakeholders

Relationships with other processes

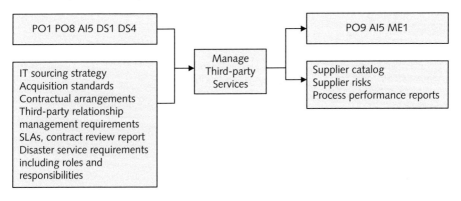

Figure 4.38 Relationships of 'Manage third-party services'

DS3   Manage Performance and Capacity
Goal

To manage performance and capacity of IT resources to ensure that information resources supporting business requirements are continually available.

Activities

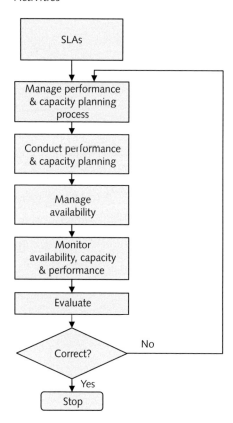

Figure 4.39 Activities of 'Manage performance and capacity'

The following activities are carried out in the IT process 'Manage performance and capacity':

- Establish a planning process for the review of performance and capacity of IT resources
- Review current IT resources performance and capacity
- Conduct IT resources performance and capacity forecasting
- Conduct gap analysis to identify IT resources mismatch
- Conduct contingency planning for potential IT resources unavailability
- Continuously monitor and report the availability, performance and capacity of IT resources

Relationships with other processes

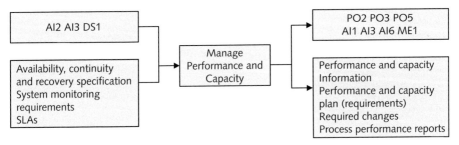

Figure 4.40 Relationships of 'Manage performance and capacity'

DS4   Ensure Continuous Service

Goal

To minimize the probability and impact of major IT service interruptions on key business processes.

Activities

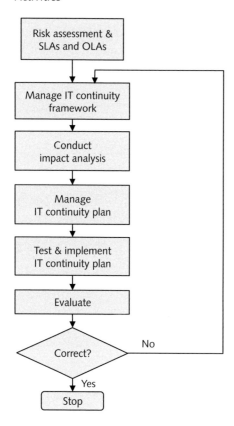

Figure 4.41 Activities of 'Ensure continuous service'

The following activities are carried out in the IT process 'Ensure continuous service':

- Develop an IT continuity framework
- Conduct business impact analysis and risk assessment
- Develop and maintain IT continuity plans
- Identify and categorize IT resources based on recovery objectives
- Define and execute change control procedures to ensure IT continuity plan is current
- Regularly test the IT continuity plan
- Develop follow-on action plan from test results
- Plan and conduct IT continuity training
- Plan IT services recovery and resumption
- Plan and implement backup storage and protection
- Establish procedures for conducting post-resumption reviews

Relationships with other processes

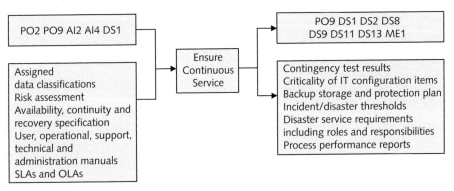

Figure 4.42 Relationships of 'Ensure continuous service'

DS5   Ensure Systems Security

Goal

To protect all IT assets to minimize business impact of security vulnerabilities and incidents.

Activities

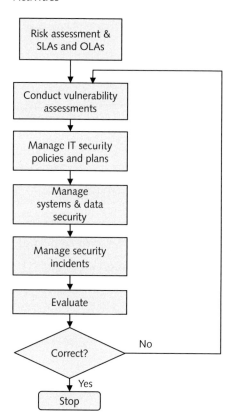

Figure 4.43 Activities of 'Ensure systems security'

The following activities are carried out in the IT process 'Ensure systems security':
- Define and maintain an IT security plan
- Define, establish and operate an identity (account) management process
- Monitor potential and actual security incidents
- Periodically review and validate user access rights and privileges
- Establish and maintain procedures for maintaining and safeguarding cryptographic keys
- Implement and maintain technical and procedural controls to protect information flows across networks
- Conduct regular vulnerability assessments

Relationships with other processes

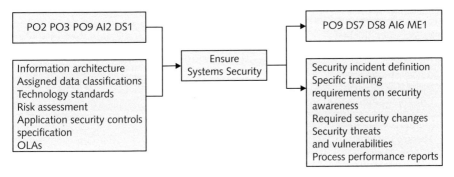

Figure 4.44 Relationships of 'Ensure systems security'

DS6   Identify and Allocate Costs

Goal

To identify and allocate costs to ensure the business to make more informed decisions regarding the use of IT services.

Activities

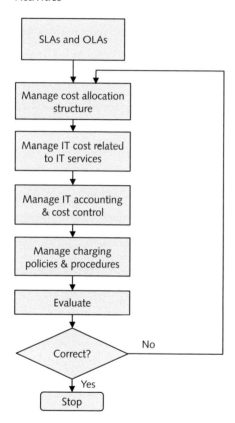

Figure 4.45 Activities of 'Identify and allocate costs'

The following activities are carried out in the IT process 'Identify and allocate costs':
- Map IT infrastructure to services provided/business processes supported
- Identify all IT costs (people, technology, etc.) and map them to IT services on a unit cost basis
- Establish and maintain an IT accounting and cost control process
- Establish and maintain charging policies and procedures

Relationships with other processes

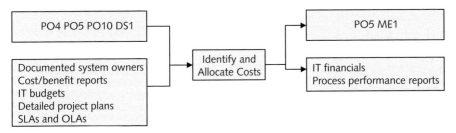

Figure 4.46 Relationships of 'Identify and allocate costs'

DS7   Educate and Train Users

Goal

To educate and train users to ensure effective use of technology and applications and compliance with key controls on security.

Activities

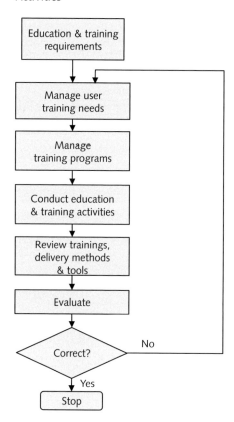

Figure 4.47 Activities of 'Educate and train users'

The following activities are carried out in the IT process 'Educate and train users':
• Identify and characterize users' training needs
• Build a training program
• Conduct awareness, education and training activities
• Perform training evaluation
• Identify and evaluate best training delivery methods and tools

Relationships with other processes

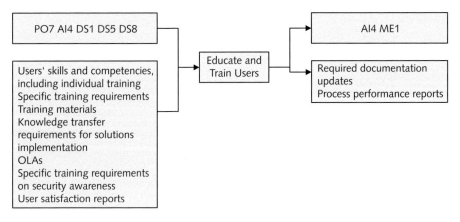

Figure 4.48 Relationships of 'Educate and train users'

DS8   Manage Service Desk and Incidents

Goal

To manage service desk and incidents to ensure a timely and effective response to IT user queries and problems.

Activities

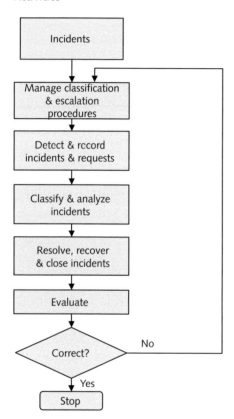

Figure 4.49 Activities of 'Manage service desk and incidents'

The following activities are carried out in the IT process 'Manage service desk and incidents':

- Create classification (severity and impact) and escalation procedures (functional and hierarchical)
- Detect and record incidents / service requests / information requests
- Classify, investigate and diagnose queries
- Resolve, recover and close incident
- Inform users (e.g., status updates)
- Produce management reporting

Relationships with other processes

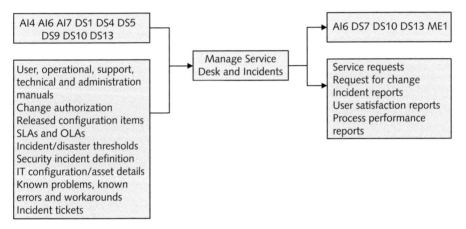

Figure 4.50 Relationships of 'Manage service desk and incidents'

[N.B. The service request as output to DS13 'Manage Operations' differs from COBIT 4.1]

DS9   Manage the Configuration

Goal

To manage the configuration to ensure the integrity of hardware and software configurations by using an accurate and complete configuration repository.

Activities

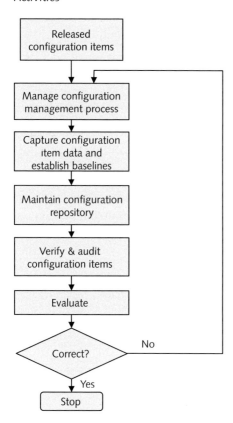

Figure 4.51 Activities of 'Manage the configuration'

The following activities are carried out in the IT process 'Manage the configuration':
- Develop configuration management planning procedures
- Collect initial configuration information and establish baselines
- Verify and audit configuration information (includes detection of unauthorized software and hardware)
- Update the configuration repository

Relationships with other processes

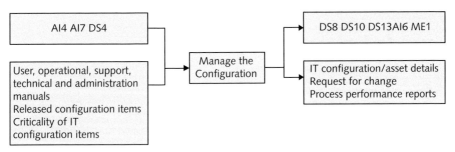

Figure 4.52 Relationships of 'Manage the configuration'

DS10   Manage Problems

Goal

To manage problems to improve service levels, reduce costs and improve customer convenience and satisfaction.

Activities

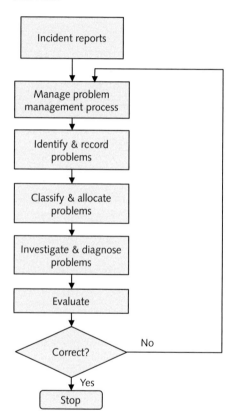

Figure 4.53 Activities of 'Manage problems'

The following activities are carried out in the IT process 'Manage problems':
- Identify and classify problems
- Perform root cause analysis
- Resolve problems
- Review status of problems
- Issue recommendations for improvement and create a related request for change
- Maintain problem records

Relationships with other processes

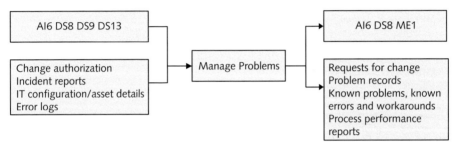

Figure 4.54 Relationships of 'Manage problems'

DS11   Manage Data
Goal

To manage data to ensure the quality, timeliness and availability of business data.

Activities

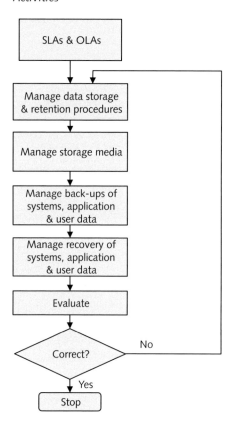

Figure 4.55 Activities of 'Manage data'

The following activities are carried out in the IT process 'Manage data':
- Translate data storage and retention requirements into procedures
- Define, maintain and implement procedures to manage the media library
- Define, maintain and implement procedures for secure disposal of media and equipment
- Back up data according to scheme
- Define, maintain and implement procedures for data restoration

Relationships with other processes

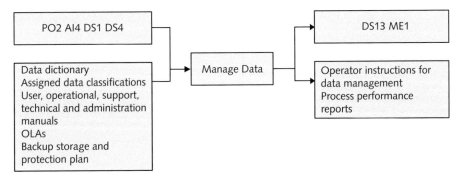

Figure 4.56 Relationships of 'Manage data'

DS12   Manage the Physical Environment

Goal

To manage the physical environment to reduce business interruptions from damage to computer equipment and personnel.

Activities

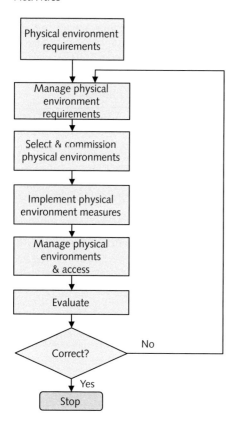

Figure 4.57 Activities of 'Manage the physical environment'

The following activities are carried out in the IT process 'Manage the physical environment':
- Define the required level of physical protection
- Select and commission the site (data center, office, etc.)
- Implement physical environment measures
- Manage the physical environment (maintaining, monitoring and reporting included)
- Define and implement procedures for physical access authorization and maintenance

Relationships with other processes

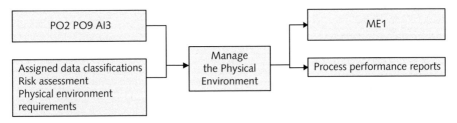

Figure 4.58 Relationships of 'Manage the physical environment'

DS13   Manage Operations

Goal

To manage operations to maintain data integrity and to reduce business delays and IT operating costs.

Activities

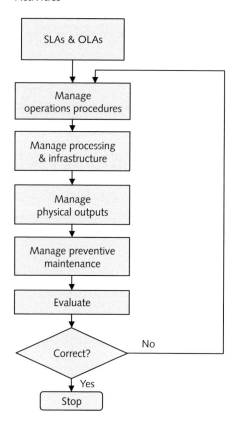

Figure 4.59 Activities of 'Manage operations'

The following activities are carried out in the IT process 'Manage operations':
- Create / modify operations procedures (including manuals, checklists, shift planning, handover documentation, escalation procedures, etc.)
- Schedule workload and batch jobs
- Monitor infrastructure and processing, and resolve problems
- Manage and secure physical output (paper, media, etc.)
- Apply fixes or changes to schedule and infrastructure
- Implement / establish a process for safeguarding authentication devices against interference, loss and theft
- Schedule and perform preventive maintenance

Relationships with other processes

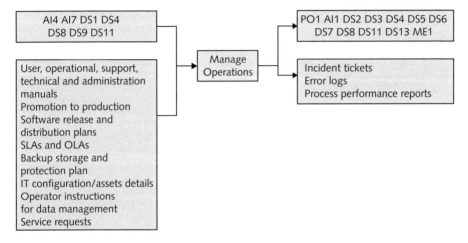

Figure 4.60 Relationships of 'Manage operations'

4.5 ME Monitor and Evaluate

ME1   Monitor and Evaluate IT Performance
Goal
To monitor and evaluate IT performance to ensure that the right things are done and are in line with the set directions and policies.

Activities

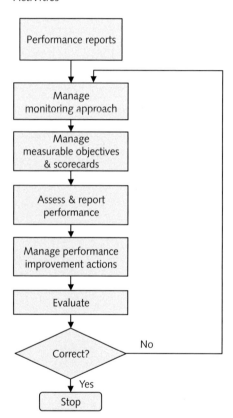

Figure 4.61 Activities of 'Monitor and evaluate IT performance'

The following activities are carried out in the IT process 'Monitor and evaluate IT performance':
- Establish the monitoring approach
- Identify and collect measurable objectives that support the business objectives
- Create scorecards
- Assess performance
- Report performance
- Identify and monitor performance improvement actions

Relationships with other processes

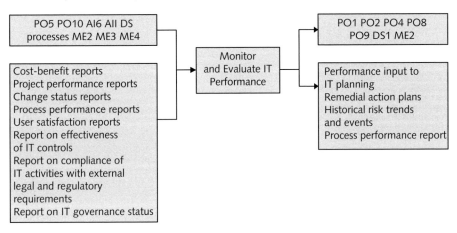

Figure 4.62 Relationships of 'Manage and evaluate IT performance'

ME2   Monitor and Evaluate Internal Control

Goal

To monitor and evaluate internal control to provide assurance regarding effective and efficient operations and compliance with applicable laws and regulations.

Activities

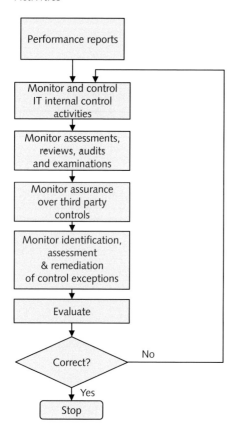

Figure 4.63 Activities of 'Monitor and evaluate internal control'

The following activities are carried out in the IT process ' Monitor and evaluate internal control':
- Monitor and control internal IT control activities
- Monitor the self-assessment process
- Monitor the performance of independent reviews, audits and examinations
- Monitor the process to obtain assurance over controls operated by third parties
- Monitor the process to identify and assess control exceptions
- Monitor the process to identify and remediate control exceptions
- Report to key stakeholders

Relationships with other processes

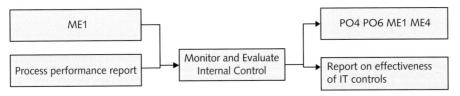

Figure 4.64 Relationships of 'Monitor and evaluate internal control'

ME3   Ensure Regulatory Compliance

Goal

To establish an independent review process to ensure IT compliance with laws and regulations.

Activities

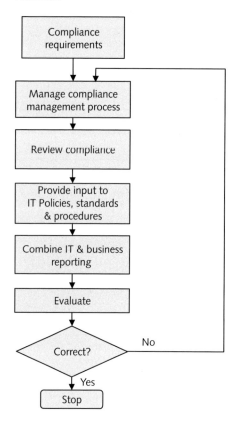

Figure 4.65 Activities of 'Ensure regulatory compliance'

The following activities are carried out in the IT process 'Ensure regulatory compliance':
- Define and execute a process to identify legal, contractual, policy and regulatory requirements
- Evaluate compliance of IT activities with IT policies, standards and procedures
- Report positive assurance of compliance of IT activities with IT policies, standards and procedures
- Provide input to align IT policies, standards and procedures in response to compliance requirements
- Integrate IT reporting on regulatory requirements with similar output from other business functions

Relationships with other processes

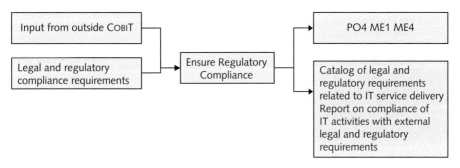

Figure 4.66 Relationships of 'Ensure regulatory compliance'

ME4   Provide IT Governance

Goal

To provide IT governance by ensuring that enterprise IT investments are aligned and delivered in accordance with enterprise strategies and objectives.

Activities

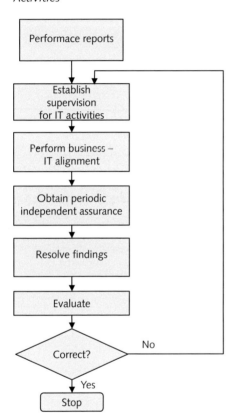

Figure 4.67 Activities of 'Provide IT governance'

The following activities are carried out in the IT process 'Provide IT governance':
- Establish executive and board supervision and facilitation over IT activities
- Review, endorse, align and communicate IT performance, IT strategy, resource and risk management with business strategy
- Obtain periodic independent assessment of performance and compliance with policies, standards and procedures
- Resolve findings of independent assessments and ensure management's implementation of agreed-upon recommendations
- Generate an IT governance report

Relationships with other processes

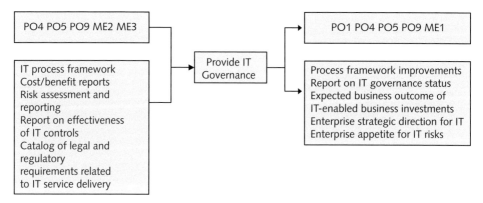

Figure 4.68 Relationships of 'Provide IT governance'

CHAPTER 5

IT Governance Implementation

5.1 Implementation Strategy

There are different ways to start implementing IT governance, and you have to find out what is the best in your own circumstances, but here are four options:

- **Maturity measurement** - You start with a workshop of two days to measure all COBIT processes at the actual situation and the future situation in two or three years. From this you will find the biggest gaps and select the prioritized processes to improve. Start with two or three processes and after the finalization of one process take another. Further guidance on maturity measurement can be found in the COBIT 4.1 publication.

- **Change management process** - The second possibility to start with is the process 'Manage Changes'. This is a crucial process in all companies. After improving this process other processes will follow as 'Manage projects' , 'Manage configuration' and 'Install and accredit solutions and changes'. Other processes to improve should be selected in a logical sequence.

- **Business goals - IT goals - IT processes** - Starting from the business goals an organization can decide the related IT goals and the related IT processes. When this logical sequence is followed you will recognize these IT processes with the highest urgency to improve. Also here our advice is to handle no more then three processes for improvement at the same time.

- **COBIT for Small and Medium Enterprises** (COBIT Quickstart) - Start reviewing these processes and investigate which ones are the weakest and start the improvement with three of the selected processes.

At the same moment organizations should always recognize that implementation of IT governance within an organization is a major effort, because organizational change is involved. Employees have to unlearn previous ways of working, move to a new way of working and become confident with it. This process has been described as the unfreeze - move - freeze cycle of change.

Implementation has to be managed as a project. Without any claim to completeness, the following project steps are required:

1. **Identify needs**:
   - Raise awareness & obtain commitment
   - Analyze business & IT goals
   - Select processes & controls
   - Analyze risks
   - Finalize scope
2. **Envision solution**:
   - Define actual performance
   - Define target for improvement
   - Analyze gaps & identify improvements
3. **Plan solution**:
   - Define projects
   - Develop improvement plan
4. **Implement solution**:
   - Implement the improvements
   - Integrate measures into ITBSC
   - Post implementation review
5. **Build sustainability**:
   - Develop IT governance structure & processes

In every project not only the tasks performed and the deliverables produced have to be taken into consideration, but also behavioural change, the communication and cultural context (preconceptions, values and attitudes).

5.2   Available tools

A number of tools are included in COBIT:
- The *IT Governance implementation Guide* contains the Diagnostics and Self-assessments.
- *COBIT 4.1* contains Maturity Measurements based on CMM.

In addition, a number of other products are available.

COBIT Management Advisor, a commercial product of Methodware, contains a database of Critical Success Factors, Key Goal Indicators, Key Performance Indicators, and Maturity Steps for each of COBIT's 34 IT processes. The product enables companies to assess an IT process and provides better assurance that key IT risks are being identified and managed.

Royal Philips Electronics developed the *Process Service Tool* as an internal benchmark for measuring the maturity of their IT-processes. This benchmark is based on more than 150 sites.

Another available product is *ezCOBIT*. This product is available for free via the website www.ezCOBIT.com. This tool can help you to investigate the status of your company's IT processes compared to COBIT. Another company that offers COBIT tools is *Meycor* with their COBIT software.

Several companies are currently working on Implementation Tools for IT-processes, based on COBIT. Other companies are working on models for health check and awareness, extending the maturity measurement to the business processes (first step for corporate governance).

ISACA offers a one-hour presentation with an overview of COBIT. This course is offered free of cost to ISACA chapters as a mini-PSS (Professional Seminar Series program) course. ISACA also offers a one day course to explore the COBIT Framework, Detailed Control Objectives, Management Guidelines and Assurance Guide. In addition ISACA offers a COBIT Implementation Course which presents the steps for structured implementation of COBIT. The latter course delivers a general guideline as an aid for implementing COBIT in particular organizations. For a complete overview of training see paragraph 3.10 for all courses ISACA is delivering with their preferred training partner ITpreneurs™. Also Pink Elephant provides a 3-day instructor led course.

Apart from ISACA, trainers all over the world offer COBIT based courses that are developed from personal experience. In the near future more products for training and certification are expected.

Trainings are available from IT Governance Network Limited (www.itgovernance.com) and InfoGovernance (www.infogovernance.com).

Terminology / Acronyms

The following table contains an explanation of terminology and acronyms used in this management guide.

Availability	The extent to which a system or service is available to the intended users at the required times
Availability (COBIT)	Relates to information being available when required by the business process now and in the future. It also concerns the safeguarding of necessary resources and associated capabilities.
BNQP	Baldridge National Quality Program
BS7799	British Standard on Information Security Management
BSC	Balanced Scorecard
CIMA	Chartered Institute of Management Accountants
CIPE	Center for International Private Enterprise
CISA	Certified Information Systems Auditor
COBIT	Control Objectives for Information and related Technology
CMM	Capability Maturity Model
CMMI	Capability Maturity Model Integration
Compliance	The extent to which processes act in accordance with those laws, regulations and contractual arrangements to which the process is subject
Compliance (COBIT)	Deals with complying with those laws, regulations and contractual arrangements to which the business process is subject; i.e., externally imposed business criteria as well as internal policies
Confidentiality	The extent to which data is only accessible to a well-defined group of authorized persons
Confidentiality (COBIT)	Concerns the protection of sensitive information from unauthorized disclosure
Corporate governance	The system by which business corporations are directed and controlled. The corporate governance structure specifies the distribution of rights and responsibilities among different participants in the corporation, such as the board, managers, shareholders and other stakeholders, and spells out the rules and procedures for making decisions on corporate affairs. By doing this, it also provides the structure through which the company objectives are set, and the means of attaining those objectives and monitoring performance (OECD).
Control	The policies, procedures, practices and organizational structures designed to provide reasonable assurance that business objectives will be achieved and that undesired events will be prevented or detected and corrected
COSO	Committee of Sponsoring Organizations of the Treadway Commission

COSO - 'Internal Control – Integrated Framework'	The COSO publication, which is the foundation for internal control
COSO - ERM	The COSO publication, which has been published about Enterprise Risk Management (ERM). *Enterprise Risk Management* is broader than internal control, expanding and elaborating on internal control to form a more robust conceptualization focusing more fully on risk.
Effectiveness	The extent to which the information serves the defined objectives
Effectiveness (COBIT)	Deals with information being relevant and pertinent to the business process as well as being delivered in a timely, correct, consistent and usable manner
Efficiency	The extent to which activities with regard to the provision of information are carried out at an acceptable cost and effort
Efficiency(COBIT)	Concerns the provision of information through the optimal (most productive and economical) use of resources
EFQM	European Foundation for Quality Management
ERM	Enterprise Risk Management
IIA	Institute of Internal Auditors
Integrity	The extent to which data corresponds with the actual situation represented by that data
Integrity(COBIT)	Relates to the accuracy and completeness of information as well as to its validity in accordance with business values and expectation
ISACA	Information Systems Audit and Control Association
ISACF	Information Systems Audit and Control Foundation
ISO	International Organization for Standardization
ISO 9000	Quality management and quality assurance standards as defined by ISO
ISO/IEC 15408	Evaluation Criteria for Information Technology Security (Common Criteria). An International Standard on IT Security
ISO/IEC 15504	International Standard on Assessment Methods based on SPICE
ISO/IEC 17799	International Standard on Information Security Management
ISO/IEC 20000	International Standard on IT Service Management
ISO/IEC 27000	Series of International standards on IT Security Management
IT control objective	A statement of the desired result or purpose to be achieved by implementing control procedures in a particular IT activity
IT governance	The system by which IT within enterprises is directed and controlled. The IT governance structure specifies the distribution of rights and responsibilities among different participants, such as the board, business and IT managers, and spells out the rules and procedures for making decisions on IT. By doing this, it also provides the structure through which the IT objectives are set, and the means of attaining those objectives and monitoring performance.
IT governance (COBIT)	A structure of relationships and processes to direct and control the enterprise in order to achieve the enterprise's goals by adding value while balancing risk versus return over IT and its processes
IT Resource - Applications	Automated user systems and manual procedures that process the information

IT Resource - Information	The data in all their forms input, processed and output by the information systems, in whatever form is used by the business
IT Resource - Infrastructure	The technology and facilities (hardware, operating systems, database management systems, networking, multimedia, etc. and the environment that houses and supports them) that enable the processing of the applications
IT Resource - People	The personnel required to plan, organize, acquire, implement, deliver, support, monitor and evaluate the information systems and services
ITGI	IT Governance Institute
ITIL	Information Technology Infrastructure Library
itSMF	IT Service Management Forum
MOF	Microsoft Operations Framework
OECD	Organization for Economic Co-operation and Development
OGC	UK Office of Government Commerce
PDCA cycle	Plan-do-check-act cycle developed by Deming
Reliability of information	The extent to which appropriate information is provided for management to operate the entity and to exercise its financial and compliance reporting responsibilities
Reliability of information (CobiT)	Relates to the provision of appropriate information for management to operate the entity and for management to exercise its fiduciary and governance responsibilities
SEI	Software Engineering Institute of the Carnegie Mellon University
SPICE	Software Process Improvement and Capability Determination-an initiative on software process improvement
TOE	Target of Evaluation

Sources

A2.1 Literary sources

Benyon, Robert & Robert Johnston. *Service Agreements - A Management Guide*. itSMF, 2006

Boer, Sven den, and others, *SIX sigma for IT Management*. itSMF, 2006

Bon, Jan van (ed.). *Foundations of IT Service Management based on ITIL*. itSMF, 2005

Bon, Jan van (ed.). *Frameworks for IT Management*. itSMF, 2006

Brooks, Peter. *Metrics for IT Service Management*. itSMF, 2006

CIMA. *Enterprise Governance - A CIMA discussion paper*. www.cimaglobal.com, 2004.

CIPE. *Instituting Corporate Governance in developing, emerging and transitional economies: A Handbook*. Center for International Private Enterprise, March 2002.

COSO. *Internal Control - Integrated Framework (COSO report)*. Committee of Sponsoring Organizations of the Treadway Commission, 1994.

COSO. *Enterprise Risk Management - Integrated Framework (COSO report)*. Committee of Sponsoring Organizations of the Treadway Commission, 2004.

Cruz, Marghanita da. *AS 8015-2005 - Australian Standard for Corporate Governance of IT*. In: Frameworks for IT Management, itSMF, 2006.

Grembergen, Wim van, Ph.D. *The IT Balanced Scorecard and IT Governance*. ITGI, 2001.

Haazen, Walter. *Choosing your IT-Scorecard Framework*. ASP.Consulting Group, 2002.

Hopstaken, B. & A. Kranendonk. *Informatiebeleid; puzzelen met beleid en plan*. Kluwer 1996.

Kaplan & Norton. *The Balanced Scorecard.* Harvard Business School Press, 1999

Thorp, John. *The Information Paradox: Realizing the Business Benefits of Information Technology.* McGraw-Hill Ryerson, 1998.

A2.2 COBIT sources

The following publications were released by the COBIT Steering Committee and the IT Governance Institute:

COBIT 4.0, Control Objectives, Management Guidelines, Maturity Models. ITGI, November 2005

COBIT 3rd Edition, Audit Guidelines. ITGI, July 2000

COBIT 3rd Edition, IT Governance Implementation Guide. ITGI, 2003

Board Briefing on IT Governance, 2nd Edition. ITGI, 2003
Information Security Governance, Guidance for Boards of Directors and Executive Management, 2nd Edition. ITGI, 2006

COBIT Quickstart. ITGI, 2003

COBIT Security Baseline. ITGI, 2004

IT Control Objectives for Sarbanes Oxley 2nd Edition (draft). ITGI, 2006
Control Practices. ITGI, 2004

Enterprise Value: Governance of IT Investments. ITGI 2006
• The Val IT Framework
• The Business Case
• The ING Case Study

IT Strategy Committee. ITGI, 2002

IT Governance Global Status report. ITGI, 2006

COBIT Mapping - Mapping of ISO/IEC 17799:2000 with COBIT, 2nd edition. ITGI, 2006

COBIT Mapping - Overview of International Guidance 2ⁿᵈ edition. ITGI, 2006

COBIT Mapping - Mapping PMBOK to COBIT 4.1. ITGI, 2006

COBIT Mapping: Mapping SEI's CMM for Software to COBIT 4.1. ITGI, 2006

IT Governance Domain Practices and Competencies. ITGI 2005
- IT Alignment: Who is in Charge
- Optimising Value Creation from IT Investments
- Information Risks: Whose Business are they
- Governance of Outsourcing
- Measuring and Demonstrating the Value of IT

A2.3 Web sources
A limited number of references is provided.

ISACA	www.isaca.org
IT Governance Portal	www.itgi.org
EZCOBIT	www.cobit.co.za
IT Governance Network	www.itgovernance.com
InfoGovernance	www.infogovernance.com
Balanced Scorecard	www.balancedscorecard.org
CMM	www.sei.cmu.edu/cmm
CMMI	www.sei.cmu.edu/cmmi

The IT Governance Portal contains an extensive links page for use by the audience to this book.

Index

ITIL Books

Foundations of IT Service Management Based on ITIL®V3

Now updated to encompass all of the implications of the V3 refresh of ITIL, the new V3 Foundations book looks at Best Practices, focusing on the Lifecycle approach, and covering the ITIL Service Lifecycle, processes and functions for Service Strategy, Service Design, Service Operation, Service Transition and Continual Service Improvement.

ISBN 978 90 8753 057 0 (english edition)

Foundations of IT Service Management Based on ITIL®

The bestselling ITIL® V2 edition of this popular guide is available as usual, with 13 language options to give you the widest possible global perspective on this important subject.

ISBN 978 90 77212 58 5 (english edition)

IT Service Management Based on ITIL®V3: A Pocket Guide

A concise summary for ITIL®V3, providing a quick and portable reference tool to this leading set of best practices for IT Service Management.

ISBN 978 90 8753 102 7 (english edition)

IT Governance

English
€39.95
excl tax

Implementing IT Governance

A comprehensive and integrated approach to IT/Business Alignment, Planning, Execution and Governance. This book provides readers with a structured and practical solution using the best of the best principles available today.

ISBN 978 90 8753 119 5 (english edition)

English
€15.95
excl tax

Implementing IT Governance
A Pocket Guide

This concise book brings readers the key points to be considered in an IT governance implementation program. It covers the key points and action lists for a sustainable and effective IT governance environment.

ISBN 978 90 8753 216 1 (english edition)

English
€22.50
excl tax

IT Governance based on CoBIT® 4.1
A Management Guide

Providing detailed information on the overall process model as well as the theory behind it, this title is a quick-reference guide to IT Governance for people who are not acquainted with this field of work.It will provide trainers and students alike with a compact reference to CoBIT.

ISBN 978 90 8753 116 4 (english edition)

Information
Security

Information Security
based on ISO 27001/ISO 27002

Provides an overview of the 'two' international information security standards. A much-needed guide used globally.

ISBN 978 90 77212 70 7   (english edition)

Implementing Information Security
based on ISO 27001 / ISO 27002

A succint guide for those requiring a guide to implementation issues, providing an introduction, overview and background to both standrads.

ISBN 978 90 77212 78 3   (english edition)